When I Am 21

Louis Mazzullo

AuthorHouse™ LLC
1663 Liberty Drive
Bloomington, IN 47403
www.authorhouse.com
Phone: 1-800-839-8640

Published by AuthorHouse 08/20/2014

ISBN: 978-1-4969-3053-8 (sc)
ISBN: 978-1-4969-3051-4 (hc)
ISBN: 978-1-4969-3052-1 (e)

Also by Louis Mazzullo
Philosophy of Education (AuthorHouse 2012)

This book is printed on acid-free paper.

I want to give a special thanks to my friend Norman Kurtin, whose assistance with the formatting made this book possible. LM

Dedication

This book, with its wishes and its dreams,
is dedicated to my wife Eileen,
who teaches me daily the meaning of love
and who always finds me
when I am lost.

11 May 2014

Table of Contents

Table of Contents for Chapters 1 and 2

Chapter 1: When I Am 21

Chapter 2: Social Goals

F 15-11

when I am 21

1. have a place to live
2. have kids
3. go to another country
4. get married
5. see my sister
0. see my parents
7. make love
8. talk to my cottage mates
9. see my long lost brother
10 be brave and stand up for myself
11. Learn to to fight for myself

1. have a place to live
2. have kids
3. go to another country
4. get married
5. see my sister
6. see my parents
7. make love
8. talk to my cottage mates
9. see my long lost brother
10. be brave and stand up for myself
11. Learn to fight for myself

M 12-5

When I Am 21

I Do NOT got NoTTing To Whis For

I do not got nothing to wish for

Introduction

My last job in education involved working for a school district servicing a residential treatment center for youngsters who had experienced physical and/or emotional abuse or neglect and/or sexual abuse, many instances of which resulted in severe trauma and necessitated treatment in a facility outside the home. A great percentage of residents were on psychotropic medication, and many had histories of hospitalization and/or problems with the law.

The center saw its mission as preparing the residents for a return to more mainstream society, for instance with family members or in foster care or other social service placements. Prior to arrival at the center, many youngsters had already been in several foster homes and in homes with family members other than their parents.

Students' ages ranged from 4 to 21, and their lengths of stay from one day to several years. Typically, students entered at 12-16 years of age, with a common length of stay between 3 and 12 months. (The average age at time of admittance grew older, and the length of stay grew shorter, during the years I worked there.)

Over the course of my eighteen years in the school district, I had a variety of jobs. One was Education Evaluator/Ease of Entry Teacher. In this capacity I was responsible for the most recent five or six students who had entered the school. (We averaged one new admission per school day.)

One task essential to this assignment was to administer an Education Evaluation to each student, with the goals of placing the student in an appropriate program or academic setting, for instance, strictly academic, or part academic and part vocational, and also to provide a baseline upon which progress in a variety of academic and social areas could be assessed.

The Education Evaluation included reading and math assessments, a writing sample and a Self-Evaluation. By means of the writing sample, titled 'When I Am 21', I hoped to gain a quick but meaningful appraisal of each student's writing skills, as well as a brief window into the student's psyche. (1)

The Self-Evaluation consisted of two parts, one involving personal and social goals, and the other involving academic subjects. I asked students to articulate goals for themselves in various areas. I sought to foster self-awareness with all students and to communicate that I was available to work with them to formulate goals for themselves. The Self-Evaluation consisted of nine writing assignments, the first of which, 'When I Am 21', was administered as the writing sample mentioned above as part of the Education Evaluation.

Typical length of stay for students in the Ease of Entry class was about one week. Generally on students' second or third day of attendance, I asked them to complete the remaining eight pages of the Self-Evaluation (four pages on personal/social and four on academic).

The aggregate of these nine papers is the subject of this book. The papers are formed into three chapters:

Chapter 1 When I Am 21
Chapter 2 Social Goals
Chapter 3 Academic Goals

Chapter 1
When I Am 21:
For the writing sample, I handed a sheet of paper to each student, titled "When I Am 21". My instructions were, roughly, "Now I'd like to have a writing sample from you. I'd like you to write what you would wish for, for yourself, if you could wish for anything, for when you turn 21. You can write as much or as little as you like, on any topic that you want, and you can take as much time as you need. If you need help with spelling, just ask." (2)

Subsections of **Chapter 1** generally begin with *Student Papers (3)* relevant to the topic, followed by *Summary of Wishes* (4), and concluding with *Commentary* (5).

Chapter 2
Social Goals:
To assess social goals, students were asked to answer one question, per page, on each of four topics:
Adult Relations: What are my goals for improving my skills with adult relations?
Peer Relations. What are my goals for improving my skills with peer relations?
Character. What are my goals for improving my character?
Citizenship: What are my goals for improving my citizenship?

Each section of **Chapter 2** begins with *Student Papers* relevant to the topic, followed by *Commentary.* There is no *Summary of Wishes* section.

Chapter 3

Academic Goals: (6)

For academic goals, I had students complete four pages, each on one of four academic subjects, with specific questions:

Language Arts:
What are Language Arts?
Why do we study Language Arts?
What are my goals in Language Arts?
What questions do I have regarding the study of Language Arts?
Mathematics:
Why do we study Mathematics?
My favorite part of Mathematics is...
My least favorite part of Mathematics is...
How can teachers make the study of Mathematics more interesting?
Social Studies:
What is Social Studies?
Why do we study Social Studies?
What questions do I have about Social Studies?
Science:
Why do we study Science?
In Science, I enjoy learning about...
I would like to learn more about...

Each section of **Chapter 3** contains selected responses from the *Student Papers*, without *Summary of Wishes* and without *Commentary.*

My plan was to meet individually with each student, once the Self-Evaluation was completed, to discuss and prioritize stated goals, to identify and list component steps necessary to the attainment of selected goals, and/or to work with the student to devise a practical plan to work toward the reaching of his goals.

A considerable body of research (7), as well as my own experience, indicates that individuals are more invested in reaching goals if they are given the opportunity to participate in goal-setting. This process is student-centered, and students tend to respond very positively to initiatives that value their opinions and their autonomy. My recommendation to school district administration was that student goals be reviewed as needed by staff (therapist/teacher) and student, but at least once or twice a semester, perhaps to coincide with quarterly report cards.

Curricular and extra-curricular plans should be directed, at least in part, towards improving students' self-awareness regarding their interests, talents, skills, and emotional health. This acquired knowledge will assist greatly in meetings to review goals, and will be especially helpful if we need to revisit and write new goals, with new component sub-goals. (8) The goals of each student are unique and personal. As we grow in self-knowledge, we become more specific, more practical and more closely aligned with our interests and skills.

A comparison of previous goals with new goals could also be useful to assess progress in language and writing skills.

My intentions with this book are

1. to provide a window into a world of youngsters far removed from the mainstream of society, children who have experienced abuse and/or neglect in their childhood and who were separated from the family into which they were born;

2. to shed light not only on these particular students, but also - by extension - on children in general, on philosophy and on education, to suggest avenues for working with our particular students to improve their emotional and social health; and

3. to complement my first book, Philosophy of Education (9), as these *Student Papers* have influenced so much of the philosophy described therein.

Both books have applications to all student populations. When I Am 21 (10) however, is more specifically a description and commentary of abused/neglected students, their personalities and their needs.

Copies of *Student Papers* totaling about 900 were gathered over the period roughly from 1992 to 2006. Of the 900, approximately 150 (in whole or in part) were selected for inclusion. However, all 900 were accounted for in the *Summary of Wishes* subsections in **Chapter 1.**

At the time I collected these papers, I did not know that they would be reproduced in a book, and some of the copies are not as clean or as complete as I would like. When copies were made, certain margins were cut too closely and a few letters and words were unfortunately cropped.

Many of these *Student Papers* are copies of copies, and it is often difficult to distinguish punctuation from stray marks. Therefore, it is generally ill-advised to interpret punctuation; likewise with capitalization, as our students often switch between upper and lower case without attention to grammar.

This selection of papers is not in any way a scientific sample and should not be generalized in any statistical way to be indicative of a population subset. This is an informal group of papers, with my informal comments and observations, and they are not intended to be scientific in any way.

Student Papers have not been altered, save to remove students' names and dates of writing. Whenever available, however, the gender and age of the student at the time of writing are included. Gender is noted in the left/upper left portion of the paper, followed by age at time of writing. For instance, F 14-6 indicates a female writer age 14 years 6 months at time of writing. If gender or age is unknown, it will be so noted, indicated by a U or simply left blank.

For 'When I Am 21' and the four pages of Social Goals, I have provided a readable version below the student version. *Student Papers* and portions thereof are presented verbatim. Spelling, grammatical and semantic corrections, noted in italics within parentheses following the corrected item, *were made only insofar as they aid in communication.*

I had to make several decisions when writing this book, for instance which papers to include and how I wanted to organize them. Another was how many of my own words I wanted to include; I knew the strength of the book lay in the students' writing and not in my commentary. And yet, I thought that merely compiling a book of student writings, without comments, would not do justice to the students' work. Therefore, I have included commentary, however brief.

I often reference Philosophy of Education. My goals in this regard are to show how student work has influenced my philosophy and to provide references for further elaboration on particular points. My intention and belief nonetheless, throughout this work, are that one need not be familiar with my first book in order to garner whatever When I Am 21 has to offer.

Chapter One: When I Am 21

The American Dream: Student Papers

M 12-0

When I Am 21

I would like to have a family
And kins, a car, nice house,
Plus a good JOB.

I would like to have a family and kids, a car, nice house, plus a good job

M

When I Am 21

nice Home a Job acar a ~~[illegible]~~ family

nice home a job a car a family

[assisted spelling: family]

M 14-3

when I 21 I wish for family
a car A Job so that I can take
car of my wife and kids and to
put food on the table and
in the refrigarator and my own house.

When I (am) 21 I wish for family a car a job so that I can take care of my wife and kids and to put food on the table and in the refrigerator and my own house.

M 15-6

When I am 21...

When I turn 21, I would wish for a beautiful wife whom I love and admire. I would have a 2-story house with a nice, bright green lawn. I'd have two children (both boys) and a dog, That would get my paper in the morning. I would also have a job as a geneticist and "mucho pesos"!

When I turn 21, 1 would wish for a beautiful wife whom I love and admire. I would have a 2-story house with a nice, bright green lawn. I'd have two children (both boys) and a dog, that would get my paper in the morning. I would also have a job as a geneticist and "mucho pesos"!

M 14-9

When I Am 21

When I am 21 I want to be financially and mentally And phisically set. I wat to have a car house and family. I would want to be finished collage and I will have my mind on my family.

When I am 21 I want to be financially and mentally and physically set. I want to have a car house and family. I would want to be finished college and I will have my mind on my family.

M 13-4

When I Am 21

when I am 21 I want to have
a job a house a wife and a
car but to ecrn all that I have
to work hard and accompish that
goal to succeed in life.

When I am 21 I want to have a job a house a wife and a car but to earn all that I have to work hard and accomplish that goal to succeed in life.

M 13-8

When I Am 21

I would wish for have a nice family, a good wife and good children and a good school for my children and good jobs for me and my wife so we could put food on the table and clothe on their backs and a nice home.

I would wish for have a nice family, a good wife and good children and a good school for my children and good jobs for me and my wife so we could put food on the table and clothe on their backs and a nice home.

M 16-6

When I Am 21

When I am 21 I would like to have a job. I would prefer a good paying job. I would like to get married, have kids, and own a house.

When I am 21 I would like to have a job. I would prefer a good paying job. I would like to get married, have kids, and own a house.

M 14-7

When I Am 21

get a job

finish school

have a house

have a family

get a job

finish school

have a house

have a family

M 10-11

When I Am 21

a car

2 Kids

a Wife

a house

a Job

a car

2 kids

a wife

a house

a Job

M 15-0

When I Am 21

Jop

Car

house

mom

girl

baby

dogs

Cats

~~Sport~~

job car house mom girl baby dogs cats

M 12-7

When I Am 21

Car
Job
House
Money
kids
Store
food
friends
goodthings

Car
Job
House
Money
Kids
Store
food
friends
good things

M

When I Am 21

I would whis for A wife A
car and a Job and a place
to live ant. Then I would like
to be happy my oland tirr life
so no one would brther me
and my family

I would wish for a wife a car and a job and a place to live and. Then I would like to be happy my whole entire life so no one would bother me and my family

The American Dream: *Commentary*

As I began to read and reread the 'When I Am 21' papers, I found that the majority of student wishes fit into the categories of job, family and home. Studying the results further, I realized that what my students wanted for themselves were the same things that billions of people in the world yearn for, namely, some variation of *The American Dream.*

The first use of the phrase *American Dream* occurred in James Truslow Adams's 1931 book The Epic of America. *The American Dream* is the belief that every person in America can achieve a better life for him/herself by working hard, and this better life includes a good job, a family, a house and an automobile.

"That dream of a land in which life should be better and richer and fuller for every man, with opportunity for each according to his ability or achievement.... It is not a dream of motor cars and high wages merely, but a dream of a social order in which each man and each woman shall be able to attain to the fullest stature of which they are innately capable, and be recognized by others for what they are, regardless of the fortuitous circumstances of birth or position...being able to grow to fullest development as man and woman, unhampered by the barriers which had slowly been erected in older civilizations, unrepressed by social orders which had developed for the benefit of classes rather than for the simple human being of any and every class."

The Epic of America, James Truslow Adams

Adams believed that *The American Dream* referred not only to acquiring middle-class material goods, but also to the ability of all persons to reach 'the fullest stature of which they are innately capable'. Adams understood the importance of individual autonomy in a person's job choice. He also saw America as a nation founded with the belief that all persons could rise beyond the social and economic strata into which they were born, a belief in the value, strength and vibrancy of individuality. Adams addresses the common strivings of humankind, and he notes that America, with its ideological values of individual freedoms associated with democracy and capitalism, is suited to facilitate the reaching of the highest potential of every individual, in other words, to assist each person in reaching the highest standard of living in the various spheres of human life (11). Adams sees a nation built in the midst of people's differences, where citizens are not all judged by the same standards but are 'recognized for what they are', for their actions and for their accomplishments. This view expresses and reinforces the highest ideals of a democratic society. *The American Dream is a dream of freedom* - freedom to work, live, travel, vote and pray, freedom to acquire material wealth and material goods and freedom to live a fulfilled and happy life.

Adams believes that *The American Dream* represents the highest potential for human happiness, namely, the development of autonomous human beings whose strivings for work commensurate with their interests and skills benefits not only themselves but also the community and nation of which they are part. *The American Dream* encompasses the physical, emotional, social, intellectual and spiritual health of individuals and of the nation.

Therefore, the vision of Adams' *American Dream* embodies our philosophical and psychological descriptions of happiness and fulfillment (12), facilitated by a democratic government fostering individual rights and liberties, and by a capitalist system that allows each citizen to rise to the highest economic levels. Certainly, it behooves us to assist students to recognize their interests and skills, and to assist them in the process of realizing such in their chosen field of work. (13)

I divided students' wishes for When I Am 21 into eight broad categories. The first six (jobs, family, home, car, money and education) correspond with typical middle-class values associated with *The American Dream.* The last two categories, abstract and concrete wishes (14), are students' wishes for what may be considered beyond *The American Dream.*

The American Dream

1. jobs
2. family
3. home
4. car
5. money
6. education

Beyond the Dream

1. abstract wishes
2. concrete wishes

Jobs: *Student Papers*

F 14-0

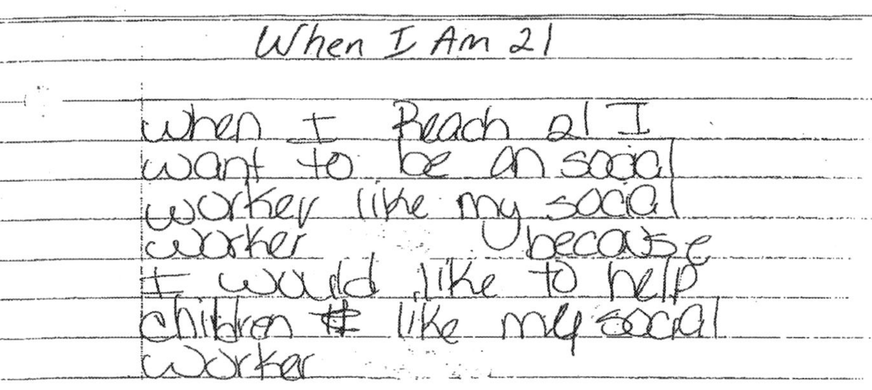

When I reach 21 I want to be an social worker like my social worker (name) because I would like to help children like my social worker (name).

M

When I Am 21

When I am 21 I will get a job as a zoologigist. I love animals. And I am going to get married. Then I will have 2 kids. I am going to take wifes Family and my family and bring them together. Then I am going to get old.

When I am 21 I will get a job as a zoologigist. I love animals. And I am going to get married. Then I will have 2 kids. I am going to take wifes family and my family and bring them together. Then I am going to get old.

M 16-4

When I Am 21

To be wokeing

To be working

M 9-2

When I ~~Am~~ 21
worker

[assisted spelling: worker]

worker

M 11-5

When I Am 21

Ta get a Job

To get a job

F 12-9

When I Am 21

I wish for a job

I wish for a job

M 10-7

When I Am 21

A JoB

a job

M

When I Am 21

When I am 21 I will like to have a job. I do not want to be on wellfare or nothin like that. I also do not want to be a bum or a drug attic. I want to be smart (get my edjucation) and get paid.

When I am 21 I will like to have a job. I do not want to be on wellfare or nothin like that. I also do not want to be a bum or a drug addict. I want to be smart (get my edjucation) and get paid.

M 15-6

When I Am 21

If I could forsee my future what awaits me what I've always longed for, I would see myself as a novice in the field of astrophisics. Ever since the third grade Ive wanted to research and resolve certain misteries in the Universe, Such phenamanons as Quasar. Black hole are bewilderin and ellude even the greatest mind of this century for someone to find out about some unknown laws of physic and the mechanism that drive such celestial being would be collosal. In short six years from now I would become what I always evied to be and acomplish the task

If I could forsee my future what awaits me what I've always longed for, I would see myself as a novice in the field of astrophisics. Ever since the third grade Ive wanted to research and resolve certain misteries in the Universe, such phenamanons as Quasar. Black hole(s) are bewildering and ellude even the greatest mind of this century for someone to find out about some unknown laws of physic and the mechanism that drive such celestial being would be collosal. In short six years from now I would become what I always (envied) to be and acomplish the task

M

INDEX→ When I am 21 I would like to be a cop. The reason for that is I like geting people who camitte crimes. I know alot of people who inspires me also.

I wathe tv the show C.O.P.S too. It helps me a little. I liked cop movies since I was little. and I still do...

When I am 21 I would like to be a cop. The reason for that is I like geting people who camitte crimes. I know a lot of people who inspire me also.

I (watch) TV the show C.O.P.S too. It helps me a little. I liked cop movies since I was little. And I still do...

M 12-7 (Page 1 of 3)

When I Am 21

When I am 21 I would like to be either a undercover police officcer; a lawyer, or a fireman. First of all I would like to be a laywer because it is a nice job and you get a lot of money and you get to meet a lot of interesting people like criminals, innocent people, guilty people, famous judges, other famous attorneys.

I would also like to be a fireman because you get to work non-stop three days a week sleeping over night and you get payed as much as a regular job would pay you and ~~they~~ there's a lot of excitement to gos with it and besides after the three days, you could get a

part - time job to go with it too!!
and get payed even more money
and you could still come home for the
weekend with your family.

I would mostly like to be a undercover cop, because you get payed a whole lot of money, you probably only need training not college and you never have to worry about missing ~~time~~ social time with your family and this is what I've been waiting for all my life, doing something risky and getting payed for it. But for now I have to think about finishing the rest of my school years and ~~gett~~ going to college or starting a new life, getting married. Life is pretty complicated, enjoy while you live, because if you don't, you just might miss it.

THE END

(Page 3 of 3)

When I am 21 I would like to be either a undercover police officcer, a lawyer, or a fireman. First of all I would like to be a layw er because it is a nice job and you get a lot of money and you get to meet a lot of interesting people like criminals, innocent people, guilty people, famous judges, other famous attorneys.

I would also like to be a fireman because you get to work non-stop three days a week sleeping over night and you get payed as much as a regular job would pay you and there's a lot of excitement to go with it and besides after the three days you could get a part-time job to go with it too!! and get payed even more money and you could still come home for the weekend with your family.

I would mostly like to be a undercover cop, because you get payed a whole lot of money, you probably only need training not college and you never have to worry about missing social time with your family, and this is what I've been waiting for all my life, doing something risky and getting payed for it. But for now I have to think about finishing the rest of my school years and going to college or starting a new life, getting married. Life is pretty complicated, enjoy while you live, because if you don't, you just might miss it

<u>THE END</u>

M 14-4

When I Am 21

I want to be a airforce pilot for the US navy. I always wanted to be a pilot because I like air-planes and I like riding on them. Also I still want to know my math because I needed for flying. Because you need to know where you're going and how high altitude you are because. there's a machine that helps you out a little but if that shut's down you got to use you head. Because If you don't know your math your getting lost because up their is just math and navigation.

I want to be a airforce pilot for the US Navy. I always wanted to be a pilot because I like airplanes and I like riding on them. Also I still want to know my math because I need (it) for flying. Because you need to know where youre going and how high altitude you are because there's a machine that helps you out a little but if that shut's down you got to use you(r) head. Because if you don't know your math your getting lost because up their is just math and navigation.

M (Page 1 of 2)

When I turn twenty-one I already want to be in the N.B.A. I want to be the best I can as a basket ball player and as a person. I want to buy a bigger house for my mother. I want my sister and brother to have the same but better. I want to help kids to stop crime so we can show the people that always looked down at us. I want black kids to have a better place to live. Instead of small tenements. I want all this to happen when I twenty one. So, in the 2000 century Blacks wouldn't be looked upon as the low lifes as now.

When I turn twenty-one I already want to be in the N.B.A. I want to be the best I can as a basketball player and as a person. I want to buy a bigger house for my mother. I want my sister and brother to have the same but better. I want to help kids to stop crime so we can show the people that always looked down at us. I want black kids to have a better place to live. Instead of small tenements. I want all this to happen when I turn twenty-one. So, in the 2000 century Blacks wouldn't be looked upon as the low lifes as now.

[Unknown]

When I Am 21

When I become 21 I want to have already taken over my moms news paper and make it to something So much better, I would like to make it go nation wite if I could, but the thing I want to do the most is make my mom provd

When I become 21 I want to have already taken over my moms newspaper and make it into something so much better. I would like to make it go nation wide if I could, but the thing I want to do the most is make my mom proud.

M

When I Am 21

When I becone 21 I want to be a garbage man becauge they make alot of money. So when I have children I can support my children so that My childre can have a education A don't haft to be like me I'm A bad little boy my children don't want to be what I been threw I use to steal, fight, curse, disrespect Adults. I want my children to be So so good in every thing good And very, very bad in every thing ba That's what I want to do when 21.

When I become 21 I want to be a garbage man because they make a lot of money. So when I have children I can support my children so that my children can have a education and don't have to be like me I'm a bad little boy my children don't want to be what I been through I use to steal, fight, curse, disrespect adults. I want my children to be so so good in everything good and very very bad in everything bad. That's what I want to do when 21.

M

When I Am 21

I want be A chemicalist so I can Make A faurula. That well give Me to Haave All Super hero AbilAty That will A vacleAble for ownlly The God Peopl..

I want to be a chemist so I can make a formula. That will give me to have all super hero ability That will (be) valuable for only the good people...

Jobs: *Summary of Wishes* (15)

A. <u>Jobs that require athletic or artistic ability and/or that cultivate such</u>

<u>athletic</u>

a basketball player in the NBA after I finish college if I can't I'll be a airplane enginer

a professional hockey player but not a ice skater a goail (*goalie)*

already want to be in the NBA

baseball player

basketball player

basketball player for Detroit Pistons

be a baseball star

be a basketball player

be a stunt man

become a basketball player

being a ball player or doctor I really don't know right now I'm still thinking about but when the time came I will be preperd I hope.

Chicago Bulls, Newyork mets, Newyork Giants

football player

football player for the cowboys

football player for the 49'ers as a wide reciever and get $400,000 as a salery

fottball star

getting ready to play Major League baseball for the New York Mets

go to the NBA and be the best basketball player in the world

hope to be a boxer I've been in boxing school for five year and I hope it pays off

I am going to be a basketball star I am going to be rich and famous, no one will be able to hold me on the court

if I do go to the NBA I would like to be with the Bulls

I want to be in the Nba

I want to play in the NBA I want to be good as Michael Jordan make own shoe and make a lot of money

I want to play pro baseball for the Yankees. I want to be the 2nd baseman

I will be in the NBA

I will soon make it to the pro's

I wish that I can be a sports player football or basketball because I am healthy and I am good at it my back up plan is to fix computer's because I always fix my grandmother's.

I wish I would be in the world wrestling federation being a wwf superstar winning the world title.

I wish to become a basketball player or a singer....I will then go on to another job after working for 5 years. I will become a wildlife represantative.J will then try to become a astranuat in space and in science
I would like to become a football player like Jerry Rice on the 49ers
I would like to have been in the NBA already going on my four year
I would like to be a boxer or a dancer
I'm going to be a famous football player. I'll play for the Los Angeles Raiders. I'll be in all the Pro-bowl games until I retired. I'll get M.V.P. every year. When am retired I'll be in the Hall of Fame, with *(most)* touchdowns ever, make it to the NBA
NBA player
on my way to playing pro Football...my dream
play basketball in the NBA
play football
play for the NBA
play for the ORLANDO MAGIC
playing basekitball
playing proffesional basketball
pro NFL or NBA
to play baseketball for the N.B.A.
try to play pro basketball
wan't to become a basketball player because you make good money and you mak real good fridens (friends)
want to be a ball player
want to be a basketbal player
want to be a basketball player and on the side a computeris like my mother
world wrestling federation
would like to be a besketball player and the Nba.

<u>artistic</u>
a good job. Such as modeling or acting
acter
acter comedy action
acting career
actor
actress
an off the books writer and construction worker
artis...or an anamater *(animator)*
artist

be a rapper or movie star
become a famous artist
children's book writer
comic book drawer
get a job in comic book companies
I am going to be in the music business like I always wanted to be
I want to be a famous writer and get reconized and respected by people of all ages
I want to sing
I will be singing Ill be so famous people will want my phone number but I won't give it to them
I will like to wish that my singing career will be on the go, and that everyone will love me.
I wish that I would be a better DJ. than I am now
I would like to be a writer a famouse writer
play in the movies
rap star
raper
rapper
rapper...for my career and my wife's will be something important like a doctor or lawyer or something,
singer
will produced my own music
wish that my music career will have taken off
work for record company, write songs, become financially well writer

B. <u>armed forces/law enforcement:</u>

a marine
Air force
air force pilot
air force pilot for the us navy. I always wanted to be a pilot because I like airplanes and I like riding on them
armed forces
be a cop when I grow up to save people's lives.
cop
fireman
firemen
FBI

go to the Army
go to the army or air force because I like to serve my country well
go to the navy for two years
going to join the air force
I am going to be a cop
I want to be expted (*accepted)* as an astrnout or a fire men because I likie adventures
I will be a cop like my mother
I will probably be getting out of the army
I wish to get a job as a police offer
I would like to be a cop. The reason for that is I like geting people who camitte crimes
I would like to be an agent that works for the government. I want to be able to take criminals off the street and my *(make)* this place saffer so there will be no more stealing, killing, rape or anything.
in military training to be a Navy Seal and on my way to being an FBI or CIA agent...prefer to work for the FBI and stopping major crimes (murders, drugs) and other crimes
in the army
in the marines so I can learn how to fly war-birds
N.Y.C. fire fighter
police man
police man or fire man
police officer
police officer for the state of new york
policeman to catch bad guys
preparing to be or hoping to be a C.I.A. agent,
undercover police officer
USAF

C. <u>business:</u>
a hotel and restaurant ownee
a store of my own
becoming a manager at a nice big seafood restaurant
boss, manerger, or maybe a salesman
have a restront and be a capenter and be baskball player
I want to own a club and a record label
making a store
my own business
open my own business
open my own dog training school because dogs are my life

own a store
own mcdonald
own my own beauty shop
own store with an arcade
well known business man
100 Larg businesses

D. career/professional/white collar:

a novice in the field of astrophisics. Ever since the third grade Ive wanted to research and resolve certain misteries in the universe, such phenamanons as quasars. Black hole are bewildering and ellude even the greatest mind of this century for someone to find out about some unknown laws of physic and the mechanism that drive such celestial being would be collosal.
alquitect designing things
architect
banker and a lawer and a backallball player
become a famous archetect
doctor
doctor because I care about people and I want to make them better
doctor on surgin. Im going to help people and save people live
fix computers or make them
herpetologist
geneticist
geologist so I can travel to study nature,
good job working in a animal hospitable
gym teacher...I would let them play me in basketball because I am the gym teahcer and I.ll do my job.
I am going to be working in real estate management in hopes to start my own buziness.
I plan on being a forensic scientist. I chose this because I love science and stuff dealing with detectives and dead people. But if that doesn't go well I would want to be a rockstar.
I want to be a chemicalist so I can make a faurula *(formula)*. That will give me to have all super hero ability that will be vaelable for ownlly the god peopl...
I want to be a lawyer so I can help people when they are in trouble
I want to be a teach because I want to help young people to be suceseful in life not,, to be a drug dealer, or a murderer
I want to be a social worker like my social worker *(name)* because I would like to help children like my social worker *(name)*
I want to have already taken over my mom's news paper and make it to something so much better. I would like it to go nation wide if I could

I will be a lawyer
I will wish I was president of the United States of America and I will make sure that nobody will run over me!!!
I would have a courier *(career)*
I would like to be a doctor for I can help people that are sick and need help
I would like to be a pediatrician because I like children and the study of medicine.
I would like to defend kids in court thats been in the system for things they really didn't do and help those who are in trouble or really need help. I just want to do all these things when Im 21 so I can show my family that I may have had a bad child hood but if I want to change I can do it but it's all up to me if I want a better life
I would like to have a ful time job as a social worker
I would like to travel to Paris for school...In Paris I can become a desiner of fashion. I can aslo become a perfeshional chef and *(open)* up a restaurant
If I can't do nothing sucessful like Nfl or NBA I want to be a bastor for my chruch.
job in computer
job that allows me to deal with adolescents and their problems
lawyer
lawyer because I like to solve problems of crime and other things
lawyer in street law
lawyer or a model
lawyer than promoted to be a judge
math teacher
medical doctor
news reporter
nurse
paleontologist
Phiysical Education teacher. I want to be a P.E. teacher because in Georgia the *(they)* look like they are having fun. So that's what I like to do is having fur
physical education teacher, for a high school
priest
principal
professional model
psychiatrist
social worker
teacher
teacher or lawyer

veterinarian
veterinarian because I got a lot of animals
veterinarian assistant
wall like to be a school teacher. In after that I wall like to be a basketball player in go to the N.b.A. in play Michael Jordan,
want to be a doctor because I want to take care of people like elederly people, so they could live longer.
zoologigist

E. <u>trade/vocation/blue collar</u>
a job at the law office
a nice desk job
a motor man on the metro north
bucter aka meat cuter *(butcher aka meat cutter)*
construction
construction worker
conductort
electrician
get a job as a helper in a hospital
get me a job at toys 'r' us
if I can't work no where sell ____________
I will be working at a small body peircing and tatooing store in the village
I will get a job as the trade I will pick
I wish *(I)* were a I ice crme *(cream)* man. I will give my mom free ice caem *(cream)* and my frides *(friends)*
I woud also like to wook people's dos *(walkpeople's dogs)*
I would like to be a macank *(mechanic)* just like my family itspily *(especially)* my uncul
licensed eletrician looking forward to getting married
mechanic so when I get strande I now *(know)* what to do
to be working in a hair salon in Peekskill
to work in a office
work a cash register
work in school
work with animals in a pet shop
worker
would like to be an auto mechanic
would love to be a model

F. descriptions of 'job'

a dependable job
a good honest job
a good job that pays 1000 dollars a week
a job
a job I like, with good benifits and a retirement plan
a job so I can eat
a job that is fun and pays a lot
a job that needs me
a job that pays good
a steady job
be at a job from 9-5 I will work hard
career
get a good paying job
go to work
good job
good job so I can support my family.
good job so if I have a family I can be supportive
good paycheck
good paying job
have a job so I can take care of my family and my wife
having a job
high paying job
high price job that pays a lot
holding a stedy job
hopefully I will be working getting my own money
I am goin to have a job
I don't know I wanna be, so many things a baseball player, a police officer, a street pharmasist, a lawyer, a teacher, counselor etc. I wanna be in the army...If I could I'd be a rapper too.
I want a job first and then I am gonna get a house and then I am gonna have a family of my own.
I want to be a house mother
I want to have a job that could pay dews for my rent, phone, cable, etc
I want to have my job
I will have a job
I will like to have a job. I do not want to be on wellfare or nothin like that.
I wish I could get the best city job
I wish I could have a perfect job
I would like to have a job

job
nice study *(steady)* well payed job
something that will make me big so I can make a lot of money so I can support my sisters,
stay home and look for a job
steady job to suport my family
to be wokeing
to get a job
very nice job
wealthy job
well paid job
well paying job
will get a job doing anything
will work hard to earn my money
will work part time and go to school part time
work hard

Jobs: *Commentary*

It is impossible to look at these student wishes and not be impressed by the desire to work. Work is the basis of community. It involves the giving and taking essential to human transactions, the fulfillment of wants and needs, the reciprocity of rights and responsibilities, and the culmination - hopefully - of an educational process that allows students to identify their interests and skills and to choose a job suitably commensurate with such. (13)

Occupational satisfaction is necessary for the healthful functioning of society. It allows the economy to flow, it solidifies the underpinnings of our institutions, and it aids the overall health of the citizens. People working in harmony to fulfill one another's needs binds the social fabric, as each person contributes to improve the standard of living of herself and her community.

Schools do a grave disservice in their emphasis on the necessity of attending college. (13) College is appropriate for students in wholly academic tracks, but for others struggling in high school - bored and disinterested in academic subjects - community work outside the classroom is indicated.

Our entire education system functions in competitive mode (16), fostering competition at the expense of cooperation. Educational competition greatly values academic achievement over blue-collar work, to the detriment of students inclined to the latter. Competition is a necessary and intrinsic component to life's endeavors but it is the cooperative spirit that enables the healthy and efficient functioning of society, whose infrastructures are maintained by a base of citizens willing and able to do physical, blue-collar, vocational work.

Why do schools so readily participate in a system valuing certain jobs and denigrating others that, although essential to society's functioning, nevertheless are overtly and covertly ignored or devalued? It is the entire world of vocational education that we are talking about here. Our system encourages students to go to college and gives the message that anything else is unacceptable. It is clear: if you don't go to college, you won't get a good job; and if you don't get a good job, you will not make enough money to be happy and support a family, or otherwise live a productive and happy life. This is a terrible message and one that is wholly untrue. Not only do we have students in college who are wasting their time, but we also have huge gaps in our labor force, filled by citizens of other countries eager for opportunities to work. Schools should be aligned with their communities as they present graduates ready to join a work force corresponding to community needs, and we can extend community to include larger political entities such as city and nation.

Many students in residential placement have had erratic and atypical educational backgrounds, often with long periods of absence from school. Moreover, many have little or no source of income. They don't have parents to give them allowances or spending money. A 15-year old student who sold drugs to earn money told me that he was unable to get a legitimate job. "Where else am I going to get money? Will you give me a job, Mr M? I will work for you." He told me how disheartening it was to be walking down the street with your girl and not have a few dollars in your pocket to go to the movies.

For so many of our residential students, it is developmentally appropriate that they earn money by working in the community, perhaps for 1/2 the school day, with the other 1/2 devoted to their academic work. Earning money enables students to see more clearly the kind of work they wish to aspire to, puts their academic education into the context of a possible future career, provides insight into their personalities and allows them the opportunity to function productively in the larger society, giving them identity and legitimacy.

The entire relationship of school to work is badly skewed, in my opinion. If we go back to the turn of the 20th century, we see social reformers advocating for more humane child labor laws and fighting for children's right to go to school. Now we have come 180 degrees, and we need to advocate for students' right to go to work.

If the school is true to its mission of serving *in loco parentis,* one of its first tasks should be to continue the family responsibility of insuring that each community member have a job essential to the running of the family/school community.

It is readily apparent to anyone who has been in a Kindergarten class how ready the students are to work. Observe the teacher ask for volunteers for a job, and how quickly and eagerly the little hands go up! Let the teacher list or picture the jobs - sharpening pencils, watering the plants, feeding the iguana, taking papers to the office - and see how proudly the students see their names next to their task. They recognize the job's importance and the responsibility the job carries. They understand that their ability to maintain the privilege of work requires the necessity of good citizenship - following the rules of the class or the school - or they risk losing their jobs along with the responsibility and prestige that their jobs carry.

Jobs help to give students purpose and importance, and they enable the workers to feel part of something larger than themselves (16), namely, their community. Partaking of the work of the community binds its members and fosters a cooperative team spirit.

Anyone visiting a school where students are contributing to the work of running the school is bound to be impressed, for instance where students read the morning announcements, greet visitors, answer phones, work in the kitchen and mop floors. Schools should expect that students be involved in the maintenance of the school. This is a message hopefully that is continued from family life prior to the students entering school, when students as children did family chores, for example, washing clothes, cooking, cleaning, taking care of the family pet, or organizing the trash and recyclables. All members ought to contribute to the work intrinsic to the running of the organization of which they are part.

The work performed by students within the school aids in deciding which students are academically oriented and college bound, and which are more suitable for blue collar or manual labor. Naturally, there is fluidity among programs as many students are unsure about their career paths. Our message is to follow your dream, believe in yourself, and work to the best of your ability. Be open. It is okay to change your mind.

Informal observations on student wishes:

1. Most impressive to me is the students' clearly expressed desire for honest work. Nobody wants something for nothing. Not one student expresses a desire to be on welfare; on the contrary, people want 'out of the system', a desire to be independent and self-sufficient.

2. Being known on TV (for instance as actor, athlete or model) is the highest prestige. This is to be expected, however carrying the danger of equating success or popularity with 'value' or 'virtue'. I once asked a group of students who their hero(es) were, and they didn't know what I was talking about. They kept referring to people they admired for their artistic or athletic skills, who were popular and well-known on television. Television serves *in loco parentis* in homes where values and virtues are not fostered or modeled by parents or parental substitutes. In these cases television carries an unhealthful parental transference and an unwarranted power and authority.

3. Many students have expressed realistic goals for jobs, for instance joining the armed forces or working 'with animals in a pet shop' or as 'auto mechanic'. Other students have goals with more complex prerequisites, such as 'lawyer', 'doctor', 'teacher' or 'professional athlete'. We ask the student to name the intermediate steps necessary for their chosen work, such as graduate from high school and then graduate from college. We analyze further: in order to graduate from high school, how many credits do you need? What exams do you need to pass? How are you doing now in your coursework?

4. One problem many students face is that they believe they will automatically change when they reach a certain age or stage in life. Moreover they do not see the connection between the present and the future. They do not see how their current habits impact their future capabilities.

5. Many students want to help other children who are 'in the system'.

6. It is beneficial and educationally sound to have high school students prepare

for themselves a budget for their expected life style for when they reach 21 years of age. Many students tend to take for granted a variety of items that they probably have never had to purchase, such as toiletries, kitchen utensils, light bulbs, cleaning supplies and household furnishings. When students have completed a proposed budget (17), we work with them to see how much they need to earn to maintain a chosen lifestyle, for instance $20/30 / hour. Then we can see what jobs they may be interested in or qualify for in that pay range. Of course, they may need to modify their plans. This budget should be an important part of each student's math curriculum, to be referred to and modified as the student grows and matures.

Family: ***Student Papers***

F

When I Am 21

I Can Be With mymom

WheN I Am 21

I can be with my mom when I am 21

M 14-3

When I Am 21

When I am 21 I wish i could
go to college And get a good
Job and a nice place where I could
live and I wish that no body in my
family could not die and myself
could not die and I wish I
could have a very heppy familly
and have a great Life.

(Assisted spelling: college family)

When I am 21 I wish I could go to college And get a good job and a nice place where I could live and I wish that nobody in my family could not die and myself could not die and I wish that I could have a very happy family and have a great life.

F 11-8

When I Am 21

wishfor My Family because I love Them
and I want to go back home

I wish for my family because I love them and I want to go back home

M 13-6

When I Am 21 I want to have a wife two children, a house and a nice Job like fire fighter, my wife as a secretary. my two children going to school. my mother would be living with me of course but upstairs in her own little apartment. sometimes she would babysit for me while me and my wife go out to the movies but I will always have a special day for my mother to spend with me.

I want to have a wife two children, a house and a nice job like fire fighter, my wife as a secretary. My two children going to school. My mother would be living with me of course but upstairs in her own little apartment. Sometimes she would baby sit for me while me and my wife go out to the movies but I will always have a special day for my mother to spend with me.

M 11-2

When I Am 21

never Die MOM

never die mom

M 14-6

When I Am 21

I wish i was with My real Mother.
Nothing els

I wish i was with my real mother. Nothing else

M 12-7

When I Am 21
My FAtheR. to be Walking a gain

My father to be walking again

F 9-9

When I Am 21
fora famaly
fora HOME
CHilDren THAT have
maners

[assisted spelling: children]

for a family
for a home
children that have manners

M 14-8

When I Am 21

I want to have a life
with a Job and good education.
I want to be successful in life
I want to be someone. I Want
want to make my mother and father
proud of me.

I want to have a life with a job and good education. I want to be successful in life I want to be someone. I want to make my mother and father proud of me.

F 13-11

When I Am 21

When I am 21 I would be an adult and I would probably have my own house and I would want to get a job and have a car. I wouldn't be someone that smokes & drinks just because I am of age to.

I would probably try to get custody of my little sister because by then she would be 16 years old and she would probably want to live with me anyway. I don't think I would ever know my brother because we fight so much but other than that My life would be perfect.

Really I think the only problem would be that my mother wouldn't be alive to com to my collage graduation and be there for me, but I think I'll be able to make it.

When I am 21 I would be an adult and I would probably have my own house and I would want to get a job and have a car. I wouldn't be someone that smokes and drinks just because I am of age to.

I would probably try to get custody of my little sister because by then she would be 16 years old and she would probably want to live with me anyway. I don't think I would ever know my brother because we fight so much but other than that my life would be perfect.

Really I think the only problem would be that my mother wouldn't be alive to come to my college graduation and be there for me, but I think I'll be able to make it.

M 13-9

When I Am 21

I would like tobecome a father for 3 children with abeutiful wife and I want to have a weatthy job and a loving wife and I want to become and loving Father like my father was and my Mother.

I would like to become a father for 3 children with a beautiful wife and I want to have a wealthy job and a loving wife and I want to become a loving father like my father was and my mother.

M 12-1

When I Am 21

I dont want be married or have any kids.

I don't want to be married or have any kids.

M 10-5

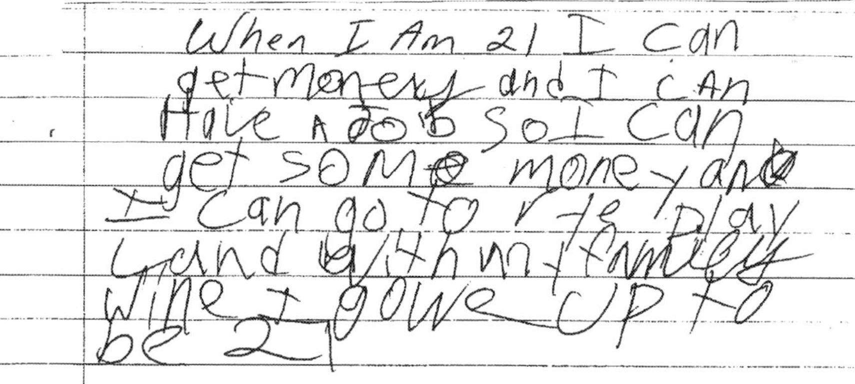

When I Am 21 I can
get moneyy and I can
Have A Job so I can
get some money and
I can go to the Play
Land with my family
wine I gowe up to
be 21

I can get money and I can have a job so I can get some money and I can go to Playland with my family when I grow up to be 21

F 10-9

When I Am 21

to get a job and have kids.
And to find my birth mother.

to get a job and have kids. And to find my birth mother.

M 10-9

When I Am 21

I will like a nice car in be a nice person I like to be a Lawyer in kids in get married help my mom with what she want in my family

[assisted spelling: lawyer]

I will like a nice car (and) be a nice person. I like to be a lawyer (and) kids (and) get married help my mom with what she want in my family

Family: *Summary of Wishes*

Family to Come:

a baby
a beateful wife and kids
a decent husband
a family and a beautiful house to live in
a family and child
a family of my own
a family, maybe kid
A family that does not argue
a girl friend that I am engaged to one child
a good wife two kids one boy one girl
a husband
a job so that I can take care of my wife and kids and to put food on the table and in the refrigarator
a wife
a wife and 1 child
a wife and 1 kid
and I want my son to be older then my daugter
at least two kids
baby
beautiful kids and husband
beautiful wife
beautiful wife and kids
being with my fieoncey *(fiance)*
buy my family anything they want
children that have maners
family
family of my own
family to support
get a wife
get married and have 2 kids
get merry *(married)*
get some girl and have some kids
have a baby a girl
Have a big honeymoon
have a good wife and kids threat *(treat)* them right not wrong
have a husband and start a family
have a wife
have at least on child and have a husband

have kids
have kids and a honey for a wife
have one child a girl
have One son and one daughter
have one son name gray in *(and)* that I will be married
have some kids a nice wife
have three children
have 3 person family of my own
having a family with three kids treating wife and kids how they should be treated
having two kids
hopefully engaged or already married to my girlfriend
I also hope by 21 to be married or getting married
I also want to meet the man I'm going to married 10 years from now and have children with him
I am goin to be mariet *(married)*
I am not going to be married
I am to marrie in a church
I dont want to be married or have any kids
I hope I have 3 kids two boys and one girl
I really hope for my family to be healthy
I wanna get married have kids
I want my kids to follow my foot steps and not smoke crack weed, drink, use dope none of that stuff and *(for my kids to)* have kids and *(for my kids to)* raise them *(their kids)* how I raised them *(my kids)*
I want me and my child to have one happy life
I want to be able to marry someone like me. Someone that wants the same out of their kids as me who has a good job as me, and who is just a good overall person who doesn't want to hurt anybody
I want to be mirred wiht cildren *(married with children)*
I want to give my child the love she need spend time with he take her out on her birthday and things
I want to have a wife and a son. I want my son to have a good childhood and to get an education. I want my wife to be happy and have a job if she wants.
I want to have 1 kid
I will be all ready married
I will get children
I will get married
I will get married and have 3 kids
I will have a family 3 kids and of course 1 wife
I will like to have kids with a nice respectfel man that well love me and my kids and family

I will not get married because she might like me for my money
I will teach my children to be more obedient then what I was
I wish I could have a very heppy family and have a great life
I wish me and my family would be the richest people in the world
I wish that I have no children if I have a child I hope I have one child
I wish that I would find a beautiful wife and also one that will not cheat or just a girl friend and I also wish that I hit the jackpot so that I will always have money for me and for her
I wish that when i'm 21, i will have a job, family, and friends. Because those are the most important things in my life
I would leave everything to my kids
I would like to have a son sow hen *(show him)* The way to life and not to be like me
I would like to have a wife and about 2 kids.
I would like to have my plans together for the early future on how or who I'm gonna have a little family of my own *(with)*.
I would like to have two kids a boy and a girl
I would not want to be married by then
I will be married have one girl
I wish to get married and have (2) kids. I want a husband who goe's to work every day and comes home with lots of money to pay the bills and child suport. I wish to have two twin boys. They would go to school and get a good education.
I would like to become a father for 3 children with a beutiful wife...a loving wife and I want to become and *(a)* loving father like my father was and my mother
I would wish for a beautiful wife whom I love and admire...I'd have two children (both boys) and a dog that would get my paper in the morning
I would wish for a nice family, a good wife and good children and a good school for my children and good jobs for me and my wife so we could put food on the table and clothe on their backs and a nice home
I wouldn't mind a child but I don't want to be married
I'll have a girl friend but wont let her tie me down...when I'm like 30 Ill have kids
I'll take my kids places
Im going to have 2 kids and a wife and be a good parent.
if I meet that right person and be faithful to him then I'll marrie him I plan on having two kids a boy & girl They will go to school in the day I'll go to work in the day & my husband two.
If I have kids I will make sure they have a good education and look presentable in school and have good higein (hygiene).

If something happened to me and wife I would like my sister to take care of my kids, evendo *(even though)* it will be a long time from now everybody has to die even me.
just want to have a family
kids
kids and a wife
live on my own with a wife and kid
loving husband
loving wife or girl friend
make sure that my family is felling all right
marriage
maybe one kide
my husband will be everything I dream of and ever wanted
my husband will love me so much and I will love him so much and will be happyly ever after together with me and my children as one big family
my son and I wish *(will)* still be together and healthy
my wife and kids
my wife as a secretary
nice family
nice wife and 1 boy and 2 girls
no kids
one baby
one or two kids with a lot of money so I can support them a wife to help me take care of the kids...wonderful family
Pass on all my skill and knowledge to my family
Perfect lady
play Playstain with my children
smart inteligent kids
some children
starting to have a family
support me and my family and my wife and enjoy lif
take care of my kid
tell my husband to get a job
to be married
to get married
to get married have 2 children
to get married with one kid
to support my wife and kids
twin boys or a girl
two girls and three boys

two kids
two kids a boy and a girl
two kids a girl or boy or twins
want my husband to have a good job
wife
wife and children
wife and two kids
wife and two sons
will be a father
will have my mind on my family.
will like a family
will like to have two kid
will want to be a father
with a nice famaliy
Would also like to tell my kids about God and take them to church every Sunday
would like to have a child, like 2 a boy and a girl
2 kids

<u>Family Born Into:</u>

all of my brothers home not in the system
at night to make my two little sisters go to sleep I make up bedtime stories for them and they seem to like it
be able to visit my family as much as I can
be happy with my family all together
be home
being home again
Buy my dad a new house
Buy my grandma a new house too
Buy my mom the house of her dreams
buy my mother a house
buy my mother ang *(and)* grandma a house
by my mother a car
fly my mother over here
for me and my grandma to be together
for my mother and father to be alive
get food for my flimay *(family)*
get my sister a nice car
give my mother some money so she can move somewhere nice and peaceful

go back home
go visit places like my grand mother visit my mother
help my family
help my family with any money problem
help my father + my stepmother out and my family
help my grandmother with rent or anything she need
help my mom with what she want in my family
help my mother out
hope for my family to be healthy
hopefully my family problems will be over, then I can live with my family and have them come to every game that I play
I also want to see my family more time than I see them now
I can be with my mom when I am 21
I can get a job so I can get some money and I can go to Playland with my family
I could vist my family and I will stop give my family problems
I don't think I would ever know my brother because we fight so much.
I hope I still got my family member to be by my side when I do something so they can be proud of me when I do it
I hope my father will still be alive. I hope my mother will get back together with my father.
I hope my mom and my grandmother will come to and stop fighting with each other.
I hope my mother and grandma be happy and be well taken care of.
I hope my mother is still alive
I just want to be happy with my mother, little brother and the rest of my family,
I mean I am gonna live in a big house and invite my mother over to live with me for the rest of her life. I love my mommy a lot and never want anything to happen to her.
I still would like to live with my mother grandfather and brother and let my father move in.
I want for me and my mom to have whatever we want.
I want to buy bigger house for my mother. I want my sister and brother to have the same but better.
I want to make my mother and father proud of me
I whent *(want)* to live with my family
I will be with me brother and mother and my sister
I will go home
I will have enough money to move me my mother and sister out of the place were we live

I will like to go back home with my mother in PA.
I will show my family how I did good with my life
I will visit my family all the time
I wish for my family because I love them and I want to go back home
I wish I chould by my mom a house.
I wish I was with my real mother, nothing els
I wish my family is still with me
I wish that my mother would be alive and healthy
I wish to be alive and with my family
I wish to see my family often
I would like for my mom to be around to see me become successful in life and to see her grandchildren
I would like to have a normal relationship with my mom and family
I would like to sew for my mom
I would probably try to get custody of my little sister because by then she would be 16 years old and she would probably want to live with me anyway
I would wish for all of my family members to come back to life forever
I'm going to live with my brother and sister because I want to go out ever day and my brother to be sleep. I am going outside be my brother wake up and look for me
I'm going to take care of my mother and father who they bring me into this world I'm going take care of them.
If I'm here I like to go home
just help my family like they help me
let my parents have a second honeymoon
Live near my ant gail
Live with my mom
me and my famliey will live happey ever avter
me and my sister will like to go home
Most likely my immediate family will be living in Jamaica by this time (my immediate family being my mother my brother and my sister)
most of all I want me and my family to see me turn 21 years old and when I get older to *(too)*
Most of all my mom to be alive when I am 21 years old
my family to be safe especially my mother father and brothers and sisters
my family to stay healthy
My father to be walking again
my mother and grandmother would have a nice house down in Florida. The rent would be payed for 35 years by me
my mother is still be alive
My mother there living with me

My mother would be living with me of course but in her own little apartment, I will always have a special day for my mother to spend with me
my mother wouldn't be alive to come to my college graduation and be there for me but I think I'll be able to make it.
my parent's is still alive
Never die mom
one of my brothers and sisters will be living happy to because I'll by them a house
One thing Im sure of though, is that I'll be living with my sister in the city. I know Ill be happy as long as Im with her.
see my freinds and family
see my long lost brother
see my mother often and talk to my brother alot
see my parents
see my sister
spen more time with my mother a *(and)* my brother's a *(and)* sisters.
take care of my family and friends
Take me and my brothers to Florida
That my brothers and sister have jobs to *(too,)* good jobs
the thing I want to do the most is make my mom proud
think *(thank)* my mother for all she's done
to be able to take care of my brothers and sisters
to be more together with my family
to live with mom
to see my family
visit my mother a lot
visiting my mom giving her money
will be helping my family
wish I would go back with my sisters
wish my mom and dad are still alive
would go on tour with my family and never come back
Would like to have my parents come live with me
Would take them to the most expensive resteraunt I could
would try to get custody of my little sister
Wouldn't give my mom no trouble

Family: *Commentary*

Happy families are all alike; every unhappy family is unhappy in its own way.

Anna Karenina. Leo Tolstoy

It is interesting to examine the relationship of the *family born into* with the desired *family to come:* children with unhappy childhoods may have a strong wish to have a happy family of their own, they may despair of having a happy family of their own or they may have an unconscious tendency to repeat their unhappy childhood. Often the child is conflicted and there is fluidity among these conscious and/or unconscious wishes. The original family becomes the template which the student accepts or rejects, which the child wishes to emulate, or from which the child wishes to dissociate. The more healthy students are those who can see both the positive and the negative aspects of their childhood, and who can accept the positive and seek to avoid the negative.

It is also interesting to see the child's love for mother (18), in many cases in spite of any abuse or neglect for which the mother may have been responsible. Many children need to keep an image of a 'good mother' (19) alive for a variety of purposes:

1. in order to maintain hope and to keep an image of goodness present in their psyches; this image and belief in goodness allows the child - as evidenced by mother's love - to maintain positive feelings of self and self-worth as well as positive feelings of the world, others, and their future, including the hope and belief that the child will be able, as s/he moves into adulthood, to become a loving adult, reverse roles, and care for mother's needs;

2. in order to keep guilt at bay; the child does not have to bear responsibility for any bad mothering, since there was no bad mothering;

3. the image of 'good mother' allows the child to blame himself for his unhappy childhood or for any family discord as he separates what is good (mother) from what is bad (himself).

Some children do not have an image of a 'good mother'; on the contrary, 'mother' has negative associations. Hopefully these students will be able to gain and maintain an image of 'good mother' through an adult figure(s) whom they experience as nurturing and loving.

Children who are unable to feel love from a 'good mother' will often wish not to be married and/or have children, frequently have low self-esteem (from feeling unloved), experience a great deal of difficulty receiving and expressing love, and thereby have unsatisfying personal relationships.

It is interesting to note the wish for many students to have their families joined, for instance by way of an in-law apartment.

In general, while information about the child's past, and his relationship to it, are important for staff to know, it is not useful or appropriate for conversation with students unless the student himself raises the topic. For most students, discussions of issues regarding mothering are generally not fruitful. Delving into the traumatic past is a journey that the student may not have the emotional strength and maturity to face, perhaps the reality of being abandoned. Nonetheless, a small percentage of students - generally older, more mature and with more intellectual skills - are capable of exploring these issues in the context of a trusting therapeutic relationship. For example, certain students may need to have their unconscious tendencies to repeat their unhappy childhoods addressed. They may feel responsible for their family unhappiness, or that they do not deserve to have a happy family.

The desire of so many students for a happy marriage and family leads to a variety of teaching/discussion points, many of which will be discussed in **Chapter 2, Social Goals.** The important piece here is to tie the present to the future, to work on social skills today as preparation for marriage and family. As mentioned in the previous section, there is a tendency for our students to assume that something magical will occur when they reach a certain age or stage in life. They do not value their time in residence and often do not see the value of hard work, whether in social or in academic areas. We must teach that today makes tomorrow. Who I am today is who I become tomorrow. There is no tomorrow. There is only today. It is very important that we teach that there is no magical transformation that is forthcoming. In preparation for our students' future potential spousal relationships, and to assist them in their goals for a happy marriage and family, we hone in on what is prerequisite, namely, their current social skills and see wherein we can set goals addressing their peer relationships **(Chapter 2).**

Home: ***Student Papers***

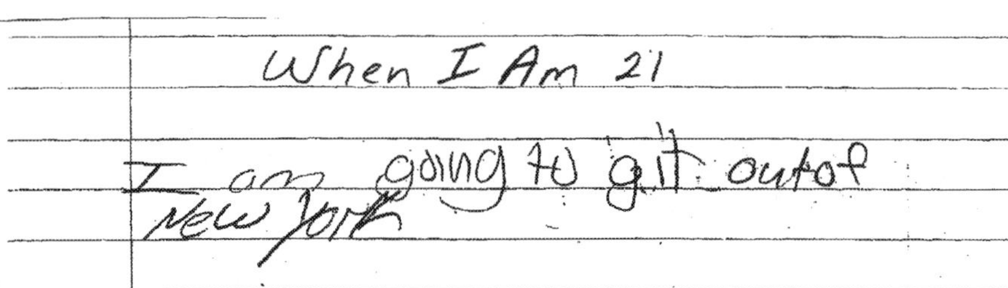

When I Am 21
I am going to git out of
New York

I am going to get out of New York

M 14-2

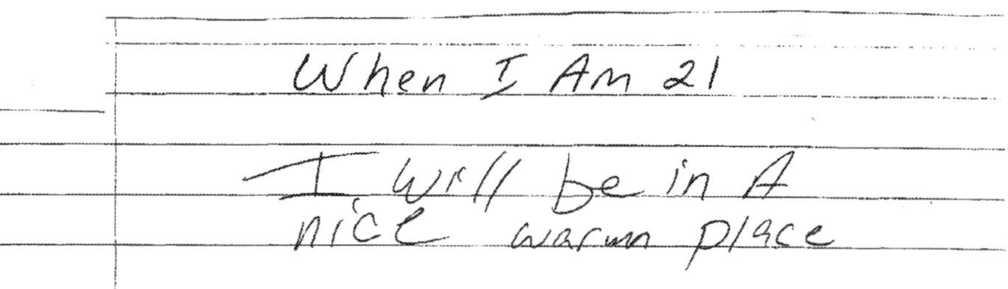

I will be in a nice warm place

F

When I Am 21

I wish to get married, an have (2) kids.

I want a husband who goe's to work every day. and comes home with lots of money to pay the bills and child suport. I wish to have two twin boys.

They would go to school and get an good education. I wish to live in a big hous with 3 bedrooms. One for my husband [illegible] me, And the kids can have there own room to fix it how they like it. [illegible] bathroom. one in my room one in each of my Sons room and one for the visitors/guest.

I want a big kichen vith lots of cabnets, a big basement for all the toys and playspace for my kids and their friends, and I want a big pool in the big back yard and a cabin for My sons clubhouse and sleepover Parties. and a big ballball coird and also my very own, [illegible] a grill for barbacues. [illegible] swing, slide and [illegible]

(My

(Page 2 of 2)

I wish to get married and have (2) kids. I want a husband who goes to work every day, and comes home with lots of money to pay the bills and child support. I wish to have twin boys.

They would go to school and get a good education. I wish to live in a big house with 3 bedrooms. One for my husband and me, And the kids can have their own room to fix it how they like it. 4 bathrooms, one in my room one in each of my sons room and one for the visitors/guest. I want a big kitchen with lots of cabinets, a big basement for all the toys and play space for my kids and their friends, and I want a big pool in the big back yard and a cabin for my sons clubhouse and sleepover parties and a big ball [unclear] and also my very own [unclear], a grill for barbeques [unclear] slides [unclear] and my [unclear]

M 15-2

When I Am 21

When I turn 21 I Want
to have a big house With
to boy a wife two cars
one for me and one for my
wife and a motor bike so
I can ride I Want to live
in brooklym so I can live
near my ant gail When I
get old I want own a store
so I can make alot of money
if somthing happens to me
and Wife I would like my
sister to take care of my
kids I would leve everything
to my kids because evendo
it will be a long time from
now everybody has to die
even me.

When I turn 21 I want to have a big house with two boys a wife two cars one for me and one for my wife and a motor bike so I can ride I want to live in Brooklyn so I can live near my aunt Gail When I get old I want (to) own a store so I can make a lot of money if something happens to me and (my) wife I would like my sister to take care of my kids I would leave everything to my kids because even though it will be a long time from now everybody has to die even me.

M 14-0

When I Am 21

When I am twenty one I hope I get and apartment or a nice job in I hope that it pays well in gives me a noufe money to get a nice job or a car or something because I am not going to be living on the street or enything like that.

When I am twenty one I hope I get an apartment or a nice job and I hope that it pays well and gives me enough money to get a nice job or a car or something because I am not going to be living on the street or anything like that.

M

When I am 21

When I am 21, I'll be in Atlanta, GA driving around in a Honda Civic Del Sol SX. I might be on the road to a successful life or I might be on the road to "Hell".

I might be a basket ball player or a football player, a doctor, or a comic book Drawer. I have alot of choices to choose from.

When I am 21, I'll be in Atlanta, GA driving around in a Honda Civic Del Sol SX. I might be on the road to a successful life or I might be on the road to "Hell".

I might be a basket ball player or a football player, a doctor, or a comic book Drawer. I have a lot of choices to choose from.

M 9-0

When I Am 21

I will get someplace
TO live

I will get someplace to live

M 15-2

When I Am 21

Plkce to leve

place to live

Home: *Summary of Wishes*

a beach house
a big house and be able to live in a nice community
a great house
a house to myself just me
all of the houses in the world
apartment
apartment on the upper west side
apartment to myself
apartnment
big house
big house for my mother, little bother, and my grandmother
big house in Hollywood
big house in Malabo with my brother and his girl
buy a big house and settle down
buy a house
buy a lot of stuff for a house
buy my self a house
condo
down south
good town
have a house in upstate a way from the City and all the Criminals
have my house
have my own home
have my own home close to my mom
have my own house
have rules in my house clean it dust it
home of my own
house
house in Beverly Hill
house in the country
house in the country so that I can have plenty of space so that my dogs can romp around in
house that is surrounded by nothing but green grass
house to live in
house with a yard, in the country
house with my girlfriend
huge mansion with a servant also
I am goin to have my house
I am goin to move to P.R.

I am going to git out of New York
I am going to have a nice house with two kids boy and a gril
I am not going to be living on the street or anything like that
I am thinking about living in South Carolina
I goin to have my house in PR.
I hope I am not living in this place because by that *(then)* I want to be living on my home with my family
I want a house, private, or to live in the suburbs
I want to live in a good naborhood
I want to live in a town that is peaceful in another state. I don't know what state now but I would want to try Massachusetts
I will by my first house with my wife
I will find my own apartment
I will get my oune *(own)* house
I will get some place to live
1 will have a giant home
I will like to live in Jamaica with my family and buy them a big house.
I would live by my self in three bed room apt.
I would like to have my own apartment and car
I would like to live in Brooklyn or Jamaica so *(to see)* my father and friends
I would move from the bad neiderhood
I wouldn't care if I had a big house or a small apartment but I would keep reptiles in one room, one room filled with tanks and snakes & lizards inside them, I would get the most exotic species.
I want a big house so me a *(and)* my peoples can live in it
I will be able to get an apartment!
I will live by my self
I will live in Gorger *(Georgia)*
I wish to live in a big house with 3 bedrooms. One for my husband and me, and the kids can have there own room to fix it how they like it. 4 bathrooms one in my room one in each of my sons room and one for the visitors/ guest I want a big kichen with lots of cabnets, a big basement for all the toys and play space for my kids and ther friends, and I want a big pool in the big back yard and a cabin for my clubhouse and sleepover parties, and my very own big ball court, slides, a swing, a grill for barbacues
I would have a 2-story house with a nice, bright green lawn
Id wont a place of my own.
I'll by myself a apartment and then buy a house.
I'll have the best house that I ever had.
Im also going to be happy that I have my own apartment and whatever I say goes regarding my house.

in Atlanta, GA
in Long Island
in Maryland
in my own house with a wife and 2 kids
in Pennsylvania in a house with a farm
live comfortable in Brooklyn, and have a summer home upstate and
a ranch in Mexico
live down in georeia *(Georgia)*
live in a nice "Big" house
live in Florida
live well in New York
living back in California
living in a aptemt
living on my own
mansion
mantion
maybe my own apartment
move to Hawaii, take my mother with me.
my house will be in Deliware Dover
my own apartment
my own home with my girl
my own house
my own house (no morgage)
my own place
nice home
nice houe in New York
nice house
nice house and everything
nice house in a nice community with my son
nice house in florida me and my boyfriend
nice house not to big and not to small but just right
nice place to live
no group home or anything like that
not live in the city I would like out in the country like texes, or Arizona
penthouse
place of my own
place to live
probably in France
rich house
to already have an apartment for 3 years
to live in a big house with everybody in my family

to live in Hawhiai
to own and take care of a house that has a driveway
very nice house
want to be down south
want to leave New York
want to live in a nice neighborhood
want to live in Brooklyn
want to live on Staten Island
When that day comes I gonna get a job and a house of my own
will be in a nice warm place
will buy a new house
will have a giant home, a maid
would like to move to hawaie.
would want my own house
20 condos

The specific place names mentioned are: Arizona, Atlanta GA, Beverly Hills, Brooklyn, California, Dover DE, Down South, Florida, France, Georgia, Hawaii, Hollywood, Jamaica, Long Island, Malibu, Maryland, Massachusetts, Mexico, New York, Pennsylvania, Puerto Rico, South Carolina, Staten Island, Texas, Upper west side, Upstate.

Home: *Commentary*

From a semantic viewpoint, we must teach our students variations on the word 'nice'. What exactly is a 'nice house'? What is their image? What other adjectives can we use? As we become more specific, we also become more realistic: we can see what type of residence corresponds with our expected wages. Likewise, with expressions such as 'nice warm place', we need to be more specific. Some goals are obviously more realistic ('maybe my own apartment') than others ('mansion'). Of course, we can contrast reality and fantasy wishes.

It is certainly interesting to see how many students seek a return to the South. We have a long history of people leaving the South to seek a better life in the North. What may have been lost, as people left their families and moved from the rural South to the urban North, is a sense of family, of extended family and corresponding family values, an image of love (including 'good mother') and family that so many of our students long for. In cities, we learn to be anonymous and we avoid social contact. In contrast, our students view the South as a place where people live in large or extended families, and where there is familial structure and support, with a clear set of values. It is a place where the elders have authority to expect that family values will be honored. In these extended Southern families, everyone is expected to work for the common good of caring for the family and maintaining the family infrastructure. The South, and Southern values, may serve as the image of 'good mother', as a symbol of mother's unconditional love. It need not be an accurate picture of reality. Its value and purpose, on the other hand, are as a positive, ideal image of family life that the student can reference in some way, as perhaps a loving mother whom she can aspire to emulate.

Car: *Summary of Wishes* (20)

a B.M.W.
a B.M.W and a 4x4
a brand new car
a car and a job because that way I can drive to work and back and a job because I need to pay for the car, you can't get something without a job!
a car for may self
a company car
a vechile
about 2 or 3 cars
BMW
buy myself a car
buying me a car after I get my licences
car
descent car would be good to have
Dodge viper
drive a lexus
drive around in my car
Ferrari
Ford Mustang
get a car
get everybody porsche
getting me a nice car
good car
have a car
have a nice car so that I don't have to take the train or bus to work or walk
Honda Civic Del Sol Sx
I am gonna get a Lexus Jeep, and take my family anytime they want to go out, because I am gonna have a nice job and that iz to be a lawyer
I want to be sitting, in a silver ck 320 Benz with 20's
I would like to be able to drive and own a blue sun roof convertible
I would like to buy a motorcycle because I've had wanted one for very long.
I would take good care of it and would ride it around to show it off all the time.
I would want a car. Because I would not have to go throw a big fuss about going to school work or other places.
I would wish for me and my famaly to b very wealthy an *(and have)* cars
I'll have a car, motorcycle and a grage to put my car and motorcycle.
I'm going to try to buy my mother a beautiful lincoln town car for the family
Id wont a car
I will have a limo at my house

I will hav car and a mortotsicall *(motorcycle)*
jeep
Lexus
Lexus coupe '99'
Mercedes Benz
motor bike
motorcycle
motorcycle for me and car for my wife
MPV by Mazda
my car will be a gold Bends with rims shinny and silver with slightly titend windows
my own car
my own car with w 21 inch in the trunk with t's 15 inch tw's in the front passenger seat facing me.
nice car
nice car that matchs the year that it is
Pathfinder
sportcar
sportscare
two cars
very fast car
want to buy a car so I can show it off to everyone
white lexus
will like to have a car
3 cars
8 cars
10 cars

Cars named: BMW, Dodge Viper, Ferrari, Ford Mustang, Honda Civic Del Sol SX, Lexus, Lexus Coupe 99, Lexus jeep, Lincoln Town Car, Mazda MPV, Mercedes Benz, Mercedes Benz 320, Pathfinder, 4x4

Car: *Commentary*

All of a sudden, we have wishes rich in specifics (gold Bends with rims shinny and silver with slightly titend windows). One might ask the students why their wishes for a car are so specific, whereas their wishes for a house ('nice house') are barely described.

We can ask students if they know the costs of maintaining a car: purchase, insurance, upkeep, which we then bring into our budget, adding to our monthly list of expenses.

Money: *Summary of Wishes* (20)

a lot of money
A lot of money in my pocket so I could get my child and girl friend what every they want
all money I need
a lot of money to take care of my nice family
a million dollars
all the money in the world
be a millionare
be rich a *(and)* wealthy
become a billionaire
give money to my sisters and any other people in my flimaly or my girl,
good income
have lots of money
having money
I hope I have a bank account because at that age the agency kicks you out and if I don't have no money I wont have nowhere to live.
I hope to make lots of money to support my family of my own and to support me *(my)* mother because she always supported me.
I want to make a lot of money lets say about a million a year.
I will be ritch.
I will be the riches man of all times
I will have a lote of money
I will have lots of money. I will give plenty to my brothers and mother
I will save up to a million dollars
I will wish to be rich and help the poor
I wish I was rich
I would wish for a lot of money in case I have kids I can take care of them and I can use the money for what I need like by a house clothing for me my girl and if I have kids,
like a nice definite source of income every year
lots of money
lots of monye
make millions
millionaire
money
money in my pockets
money to put my kid through college
most of all I want money!
"mucho pesos"!

rich
richer than Michael Jackson
richest person that ever step foot on earth
the most important thing money
the richices person in the world
to be rich
want to be a millionare
will be a millionaire
will have a lot of money
win a lot of money
2000 dolaers

Money: *Commentary*

We have the gamut here, from the virtuous 'money to put my kid through college' and 'wish to be rich to help the poor', to the sublime 'all the money in the world'. Proceeding from previous sections on jobs and cars, it certainly appears worthwhile to expand upon the discussion of wages and to examine more carefully the expenses necessary in raising a family and maintaining a certain lifestyle. Besides the more obvious monthly bills (rent, food, utilities, transportation, clothing), we could discuss expenses such as a savings fund, insurance for life, automobile, home and health, and the expenses of raising a child. This discussion is suitable for a group, as members contribute information based on individual experiences. Some students will feel overwhelmed; others, hopefully, will find motivation to work toward an occupation that can help to provide a satisfactory standard of living.

Our students have generally had little, if any, experience saving money. From the previous section on jobs, we would hope that most students - certainly by the time they are in high school - are earning money and learning to work with a budget that optimally includes savings. Classes could model saving money in a variety of ways, such as collecting pennies, or selling goods or services. Schools should be structured so that classes are encouraged to have a budget, to make money, and to save money. (21) Money skills should be an important part of the math curriculum for all students, covering topics such as savings, banks, interest, credit, wages and taxes.

F 14-10

When I Am 21

When I become 21 I would like to be in my third year of college at Prat Art institute in Brooklyn. I would like to be working in a hair salon in Peekskill. I would like to have alot of credit cards; and money.
When I'm 21 I would like to be doing everything people said I couldn't do.

When I become 21 I would like to be in my third year of college at Prat Art Institute in Brooklyn. I would like to be working in a hair salon in Peekskill. I would like to have a lot of credit cards; and money. When I'm 21 I would like to be doing everything people said I couldn't do.

F 16-5

WHEN I AM 21

HOPEFULLY AT AGE 21 I WILL BE FRESH OUT OF COLLEGE (THAT WOULD BE NYU)

I WILL BE WORKING AT A SMALL BODY PEIRCING AND TATOOING STORE IN THE VILLAGE AND ~~MAKING A SUBSTANTIAL INCOME, NOT TO MENTION~~ PLAYING WITH MY BAND - COLLECTIVELY MY INCOME WILL BE MORE THAN ADEQUATE TO SUPPORT MY MODEST STYLE OF LIVING AND MY ART

ON TUESDAYS AND THURSDAYS I WILL READ AND LISTEN TO POETRY AT SMALL BOHEMIAN NIGHTCLUBS, WHERE EVENTUALLY I WILL MEET THE MAN OF MY DREAMS.

HE WILL MOVE INTO MY SPACIUS LOFT APARTMENT WHICH IS CONVIENTLY LOCATED RIGHT AROUND THE CORNER, AND WE'LL LIVE HAPPILY EVER AFTER

Hopefully at age 21 I will be fresh out of college (that would be NYU) I will be working at a small body piercing and tatooing store in the village and playing with my band - collectively my income will be more than adequate to support my modest style of living and my art

On Tuesdays and Thursdays I will read and listen to poetry at small Bohemian night dubs, where eventually I will meet the man of my dreams.

He will move into my spacious loft apartment which is conveniently located right around the corner, and we'll live happily ever after

When I Am 21

When I am twenty-one I plan to be in my junior year of college (where inparticular I'm not sure). Hopefully I'll have a partime job inbetween school hours. Depending on where I'm going to college and what my monetary situation is I'll either be staying in a dorm or renting an apartment with roomates. Most likely my immediate family will be living in Jamaica by this time (my immediate family being my mother my brother and my sister). I would like to think I'll still have a girlfriend, as well as a personal and social life.

(Page 2 of 2)

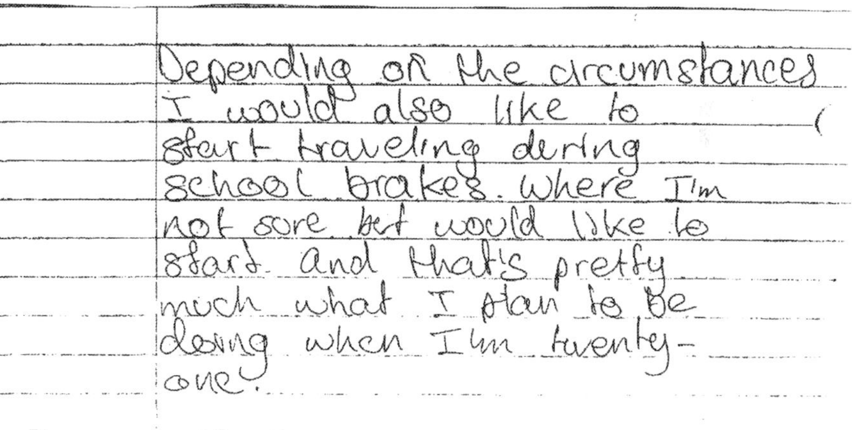

Depending on the circumstances I would also like to start traveling during school brakes. Where I'm not sure but would like to start and that's pretty much what I plan to be doing when I'm twenty-one.

When I am twenty-one I plan to be In my junior year of college (where in particular I'm not sure). Hopefully I'll have a partime job in between school hours. Depending on where I'm going to college and what my monetary situation is I'll either be staying in a dorm or renting an apartment with roomates. Most likely my immediate family will be living in Jamaica by this time (my immediate family being my mother my brother and my sister). I would like to think I'll still have a girlfriend, as well as a personal and social life. Depending on the circumstances I would also like to start traveling during school brakes. Where I'm not sure but would like to start. And that's pretty much what I plan to be doing when I'm twenty-one.

M 14-7

When I Am 21

When I am twenty one I would like to have completed my college or going IN to College. have my house, car, and job. No kids, and no criminal record.

When I am twenty one I would like to have completed my college or going into college, have my house, car, and job. No kids, and no criminal record.

M 13-2

When I Am 21

When I am 21 I do not know what I want to be, but I could see myself in a good school. I will try to be a very responsible person. When I am twenty-one I will still be trying to enjoy life.

The End
Finished

When I am 21 I do not know what I want to be but I could see myself in a good school. I will try to be a very responsible person. When I am twenty-one I will still be trying to enjoy life.

The End
Finished

M 14-6

When I Am 21

When I'm 21 I will Be out of Trade school and starting my Life. I will get a JOB as The Trade I will pick, and get my own appartment. I wont hafe to worry about were I'm going Because I will Be and adult no group home or any Thing like that I will Live my Life I will show my family how I Did good with my Life.

When I'm 21 I will be out of trade school and starting my life. I will get a job as the trade I will pick, and get my own appartment. I wont have to worry about where I'm going because I will be an adult no group home or anything like that. I will live my life I will show my family how I did good with my life.

F 15-6

When I Am 21

When I'm 21 years old, I would want to just start over of my life. I want to be in college already studing medicine to become a doctor. I want to live in a town that is peaceful in another state. I don't know what state now but I would want to try Massachusetts. I also want to meet the man I'm going to married 10 years from now and have children with him. So when my life is all straighten up, I'll be so happy that nothing could make me depress again.

When I'm 21 years old, I would want to just start over of my life. I want to be in college already studying medicine to become a doctor. I want to live in a town that is peaceful in another state. I don't know what state now but I would want to try Massachusetts. I also want to meet the man I'm going to (be) married (to) ten years from now and have children with him. So when my life is all straightened up, I'll be so happy that nothing could make me depressed again.

F (Page 1 of 2)

When I Am 21

I hope to be in college ~~studing~~ studying very hard. I hope to be able to reach my Goal and getting the highest Degree's I can get. I also hope by 21 to be Married or [illegible] getting Married. I also hope to have gottan my regular Education [illegible] deploma. Please excuse my spelling.

I hope to have my own apartment.

To be in Shape to be healthy & happy. I hope to be more Together with my family. I wonna Major in law and minor in acting. I really like learning new things. I wonna be able to learn and make money. I also hope to stay away from trouble. I also hope trouble dose not find me. I hope to be on my way to a [illegible] succesful life. I hope also my exama is gone or very un noticable. I also hope to have nice things and good hair. I really hope for my family to be healthy. I Just wonna be succesful.

(Page 2 of 2)

I hope to be in college studying very hard. I hope to be able to reach my goal and getting the highest degrees I can get. I also hope by 21 to be married or getting married. I also hope to have gottan my regular education deploma. Please excuse my spelling. I hope to have my own apartment. To be in shape to be healthy & happy. I hope to be more together with my family. I wanna major in law and minor in acting. I really like learning new things. I wanna be able to learn and make money. I also hope to stay away from trouble. I also hope trouble does not find me. I hope to be on my way to a succesful life. I hope also my eczema is gone or very un noticable. I also hope to have nice things and good hair. I really hope for my family to be healthy. I just wanna be succesful.

F 13-5

When I Am 21

I'm finished college with my husband that I have now that he is educated and he's settled down. I become a FBI agent. My mom is going to let me go on my own. I also hope it isn't hard getting this job. I have a different point of view about other people. That kids my age now saw life the way I did they also become mature at a young age. Cause if the world is tough now its going to be drama a kid is going to have to go through. That the world changes it don't have to be such bad problems that parents have to put they kid in the system!

I'm finished college with my husband that I have now that he is educated and he's settled down. I become a FBI agent. My mom is going to let me go on my own. I also hope it isn't hard getting this job. I have a different point of view about other people. That kids my age now saw life the way I did they also become mature at a young age. Cause if the world is tough now it's going to be a drama a kid is going to have to go through. That the world changes it don't have to be such bad problems that parents have to put their kids in the system!

F 15-9

When I Am 21

When I am 21 I would be in my last year of college at C.W. Post I will have many medals for track, Maybe even have a job. One thing I'm sure of though, is that I'll be living with my sister in the city. I know I'll be happy as long as I'm with her.

When I am 21 I would be in my last year of college at C.W. Post. I will have many medals for track, maybe even have a job. One thing I'm sure of though, is that I'll be living with my sister in the city. I know I'll be happy as long as I'm with her.

M 12-11

When I Am 21

When I am 21 years old I wish I Graudate Wait from Gollage and go on to pro NFl or NBA a and help my GrandMother with rent or anything she need or Be a rapper or Movie star and Just help my fainly like they help we. I Want to be success ful and do something and not Be a gangster I want to gradute and do something sucess ful. If i can't do nothing sucess ful like Nfl or NBa I want to Be a Bastor for my chruch.

When I am 21 years old I wish I graduate from college and go on to pro NFL or NBA and help my grandmother with rent or anything she needs or be a rapper or movie star and just help my family like they help me. I want to be successful and do something and not be a gangster. I want to graduate and do something successful, if I cant do nothing successful like NFL or NBA I want to be a pastor for my church.

Education: *Summary of Wishes*

a degree for machinery
a dope university
a school deplonmia
an education
be finish with college
be going on my last year of collage
By the time I am 21 I want to be in my 3rd year of college hopefully playing football. I want to be a starter and have a full scholarship,
college degree
degree in school
doing my 4th year of law school
Ervine College in California
finish school
First of all I want to get my education then get a career
get out of the group home system go to college
get some sort of college or trade, to get this job I'm talking about.
getting the highest degrees I can get
go to college
go to college and to law school and be a lawer.
go to college and study to be a secrtary
go to school and work with student
go to trade school to be a mechanic
going to college
go to school for baketball
go to school part time
Havard Law School...studying to become a lawyer
have a good education
have a masters in a trade. At that point in time I would like to be going to school still so that I can make something or someone of myself and have a little good job on the side. I would also like to keep up with my artistic skills.
hope to be a Jr. in college. The college I wish to attend I don't know.
Hopefully at age 21 I will be fresh out of college (that would be NYU) hoping
to finish school
I also hope to have gottan my regular education deploma
I always wanted to go to college in North Carolina
I do not know what I want to be, but I could see myself in a good school.
I don't really plan on going to college. But in the long run something like that may come up and the first opportunity that comes I'm gonna take it.
I have plans to be in college, hopefully just finishing getting my buziness/real estate degree trying to move on to my masters.

I hope I will be in college on my way to medical school

I hope to be in college by then getting a GPA average of 3.5. Taking part in my high school Alumni Program

I hope to be in college studying very hard. I hope to be able to reach my goal and getting the highest degree's I can get

I hope to be in my second or third year in college.

I hope to finish college

I like to finish high school + collage

I wanna major in law and minor in acting

I plan to be in my junior year of college (where in particular I'm not sure).

Hopefully I'll have a partime job in between school hours. Depending on where I'm going to college and what my monetary situation I'll either be staying in a dorm or renting an apartment with roomates.

I want to be finishing college and going to the NBA and play profesinal basket ball and play for the Orlando Magic that's my dream to play for the NBA

I want to be in college already studing medicine to become a doctor.

I want to be in the university of illinois or university of North cariliona. Playing for the tar heels.

I will be in college study for hair and been *(being)* a teacher

I will still be in college trying to get my education and working on getting into med school so that I can be a children's doctor

I wish to probably be in college taking a math course and a social studies course.

I would be a senior in college basketball getting ready to go to the NBA and having my second choice an accountant or a regular business man if basketball doesn't fall through for me.

I want my diploma

I want to be educated go to college

I want to be in college already studying medicine to become a doctor

I want to be on a college football team

I want to finish college with a degree in medical

I want to go to college so I can be on the foot ball team and if I am good enough I will go to the NFL to play.

I want to gradute and do something sucessful

I want to keep up with basketball. go to schools that have basketball in it. Hopefully I will have scholarships for basketball, so I can get into good schools.

I don't want to mess up my life and not be in school.

I whould of graduate collage *(would have graduated college)* already. I will be a college graduet and a smart man.

I will be out of trade school and starting my life
I wish I have already graduated from college
I would like to be a basketball college player
I would like to be in my last year of college at C.W.Post. I will have many medals for track, maybe even have a job.
I would like to go to Artistic College so I could get my degrees in order to become a world renowned artist because I love to draw things and it's a fun thing to do. You could have fun and paid at the same time.
I would like to go for my masters degree
I would like to have a college degree
I would like to have completed college or going into college
I would like to finish school and be a nurse, and go to school at night If not I'll probably be in college if not pushing weigh on the block.
I'll be going to colige
I'll be in my third year in college
I'll have my masters degree in Advertising just in case I need a lot of money
I'm glad Im probably going to be in college and having a part time job.
I'm going to have to study more math because everything is easy
major in astronomy that's another dream I have,
may just *(be)* getting out of college
my dreams are to finish college and go to medical school while in medical school I want to work as a beautician,
my goal is to go to Duke collage
pass high school get trainig is *(in)* computer and buisness
playing college ball for North Caralina and ... about to get drafted to Chicgo Bulls
preparing for college
probably go to collage
still be in college
studying for an architect
The most important thing for me to do is go to college and get my diploma, my masters degree, and a good education 'cause without and *(an)* education you won't be able to get non of the things you might have dream about when you were a little kid
to be finishing college
to be in college
to be in my last year of college
to be whell educated
to finish school
to finish school, high school and college (Masters)

to go to school
to graduate from college
to have already graduated
wanna major in law, minor in acting
want to go to college
want to have my diploma
when I grow I hopefully will be in college where I can learn from and from there I will decide what I am going to do with the rest of my life,
will be still in collage
would like to be a basketball player in collage and finish school
would like to be in college majoring in engineering
would like to be in my third year of college at Prat Art Institute in Brooklyn
would like to go to college and be out of high school
would like to graduate from a miatary (*military*) school
would like to have a car and my education
would wish to finish school

Schools named: Pratt Institute, Irvine College in California, North Carolina, Duke, C.W. Post, University of Illinois, Harvard Law School, NYU

Education: *Commentary*

High schoolers learn a great deal by visiting colleges. Is the college friendly? Is the campus inviting and clean? What do we notice? What questions do I have? Structured visits to local four-year and community colleges are advisable for many students. They should be encouraged, when practical, to sit in on classes, or go to extra-curricular events such as basketball games. While on campus, they should be encouraged to ask questions of students and staff in a structured setting, an activity that may require pre-planning. My experience is that many students feel inadequate as they compare themselves to the college students they see or as they reflect upon gaps in their own education. In any case, the college visit will be a learning experience, either to motivate students to pursue higher education or for students to feel that maybe they are not ready, at this time, for the academic rigor required for college.

Beyond the Dream

Abstract wishes: *Student Papers*

M 14-0

When I Am 21

When I Am 21 I would wish to have lots of money, a job, and I life. I wish that I could good things, and not bad. When I grow I hopefully will be college where I can learn from and from there I will decide what I am going to do with my life. When I turn 21 I want to have a job and go to school at the same time. What I mean by having a life is getting my shelf together and be very smart. To love and care for another, but in order to do so, I must love my shelf first to love any body else.

When I am 21 I would wish to have lots of money, a job, and a life. I wish that I could (do) good things and not bad. When I grow I hopefully will be in college where I can learn from and from there I will decide what I am going to do with my life. When I turn 21 I want to have a job and go to school at the same time. What I mean by having a life is getting myself together and be very smart. To love and care for another, but in order to do so, I must love myself first to love anybody else.

M 12-7

When I Am 21

When I turn twenty one I wish the world Will Be a Better place not only for myself But for my Children and my family. I wish I can get a education and be Somebody. I wish that I can make a Contribution to this world, but most of all I wish for my mother to get Better from her disease.

When I turn twenty one I wish the world will be a better place not only for myself but for my children and my family. I wish I can get a education and be somebody. I wish that I can make a contribution to this world, but most of all I wish for my mother to get better from her disease.

When I Am 21 I want to be able to say that my childhood and teenage hood didn't go to waste. I want to be able to say I had fun with my friends, and finished high sch (AT LEAST) at the same time.

When I am 21 I want to be able to have the knowledge and know how to be on my own, and have a well paying job so I could support myself without anyones help. I want to be able to be in a good relationship if not married. I want to be able to marry someone like me. Someone that wants the same out of their kids as me who has a good job as me, and who is just a good overall person who dosen't want to hurt anybody. Thats about it. I'm not about dreams I'm just a simple person who wants simple things, and hopefully I'll be able to get what I want out of life now and when I get older.

I want to be able to say that my childhood and teenage hood didn't go to waste. I want to be able to say I had fun with my friends, and finished high school (AT LEAST) at the same time.

When I am 21 I want to be able to have the knowledge and know how to be on my own, and have a well paying job so I could support myself without anyone's help. I want to be able to be in a good relationship if not married. I want to be able to marry someone like me. Someone that wants the same out of their kids as me who has a good job as me, and who is just a good overall person who doesn't want to hurt anybody. That's about it. I'm not about dreams I'm just a simple person who wants simple things, and hopefully I'll be able to get what I want out of life now and when I get older.

F

When I Am 21

The only thing that I wish For, is to be alive and happy. To me, nothing is important over then being here on earth. There a lot OF great things on earth and a lot that I would like to achieve. So I wish For life and true happiness.

The only thing that I wish for, is to be alive and happy. To me, nothing is important over than being here on earth. There (are) a lot of great things on earth and a lot that I would like to achieve. So I wish for life and true happiness.

M 11-3

When I Am 21

I woual d wish for great wisdom I would wish for no wars. I would wish for a lot of friends. I would wish for a lot of money.

I would wish for great wisdom. I would wish for no wars. I would wish for a lot of friends. I would wish for a lot of money.

M 14-10

When I Am 21

To go on a talk show and find my lost Girlfriend who moved to washinton. I wish for this 'cause I loved her with all my heart and when she left I couldn't say good-bye

To go on a talk show and find my lost girlfriend who moved to Washington I wish for this 'cause I loved her with all my heart and when she left I couldn't say good-bye

F 15-8

When I Am 21

When I am twentyone I want to have my own house. I want to go to college and study to be a secrtary. I want to take Dance Classes so I can become a professional dancer in hip-hop. I also want to help kids with their self in how hard life is when you don't know your feelings and how you feel about thing. I also want to help the poor give money when I have, try and have a extra bathtube and up stairs in my house so they can shower I can give them something to eat and let them start fresh let them get a job and do the right them for them selves go back to school.

When I am twenty one I want to have my own house. I want to go to college and study to be a secretary. I want to take dance classes so I can become a professional dancer in hip-hop. I also want to help kids with their self in how hard life is when you don't know your feelings and how you feel about things. I also want to help the poor give money when I have, try and have a extra bathtub upstairs in my house so they can shower I can give them something to eat and let them start fresh let them get a job and do the right thing for themselves go back to school.

F 9-3

When I Am 21

I am free at last

I am free at last

F

When I Am 21

When I am 21 I hope to have all my goals for my life accomplished. In other words I hope to have my life together. Some examples of these things are having a car, being well along in my college and having a good job. I also hope by then I can spend more time with my family and friends. I will probley think back on the time I spent being tortured at and reflect on what it is really like in the real world. When I am 21 all I wish for in a nutshell is happiness, good health, family and good friends.

When I am 21 I hope to have all my goals for my life accomplished. In other words I hope to have my life together. Some examples of these things are having a car, being well along in my college and having a good job. I also hope by then I can spend more time with my family and friends. I will probably think back on the time I spent being tortured at [name of residential center] and reflect on what it is really like in the real world. When I am 21 all I wish for in a nutshell is happiness, good health, family and good friends.

M 13-6

When I Am 21

When I am 21 I will make a difference.
When I am 21 I will make something of my self
When I am 21 I will be famous
When I am 21 I will be a father
When I am 21 I will be somebody
When I am 21 I will be a rolemodel
When I am 21 I will be a millionaire (Hopefully).
When I am 21 I will look back and laugh
When I am 21 I will help the needy

I got a long way till 21 hopefully I will make it.

(Assisted spelling: difference needy model bumpy)

When I am 21 I will make a difference.
When I am 21 I will make something of myself
When I am 21 I will be famous
When I am 21 I will be a father
When I am 21 I will be somebody
When I am 21 I will be a role model
When I am 21 I will be a millionaire (Hopefully).
When I am 21 I will look back and laugh
When I am 21 I will help the needy

I got a long way till 21 hopefully I will make it.

When I Am 21

I want to go back to my flamiy I Love them also I want a good Job in the City maby a Scientist and Study Planets anid makea discovery I laso want t be the frist person on mars I have a teacher my old teacher he like planets too. his name is [illegible] he said in ten nine years People well astronauts will be going to mars. I want to be that Pearson in a Space Ship going to mars. and then what we will do is but oxygen on it mars has co2 and we will but plants too make Oxgen anc if we can't Becase there a dirkent gas on mars we will pump carbon Dioxide and put plants tomake oxygen. then go back to earth and help my flamx and buy them prensnts and mak them happy,

I want to go back to my family I love them also I want a good job in the city maybe a scientist and study planets and make a discovery I also want to be the first person on Mars I have a teacher my old teacher he likes planets too. His name is (name of teacher). He said in ten or nine years people (as) well (as) astronauts will be going to Mars. I want to be that person in a space ship going to Mars. And then what we will do is put oxygen on it Mars has CO2 and we will put plants to make oxygen and if we can't because there is a different gas on Mars we will pump carbon dioxide and put plants to make oxygen. Then go back to earth and help my family and buy them present(s), and make them happy.

M 13-10

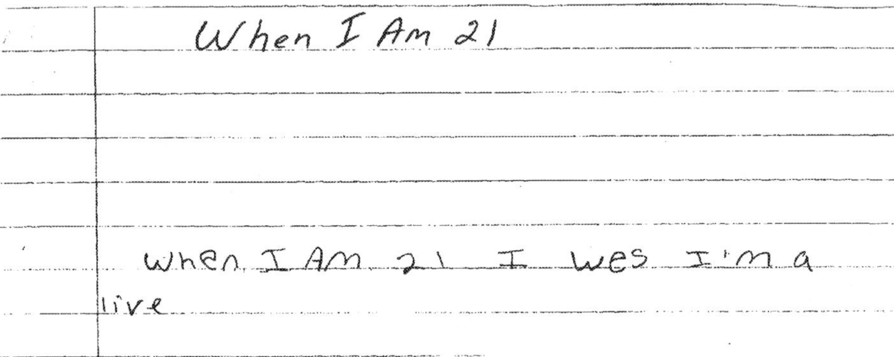
When I Am 21

When I Am 21 I wes I'm a live

When I am 21 I wish I'm alive

M 15-5

When I Am 21

I want to get away from

everything & everyone -

I want to get away from everything & everyone -

M

When I Am 21

I want to be a famous writer and get reconized and respected by people of all age I would like to have a boy Beagle dog; to keep me from being lonely and have my spirit high. I would like to be able to drive and own a blue sunroof convertable; and to own and take care of a house that has a driveway.

I want to be a famous writer and get recognized and respected by people of all ages. I would like to have a boy beagle dog; to keep me from being lonely and have my spirits high. I would like to be able to drive and own a blue sunroof convertible; and to own and take care of a house that has a driveway.

M

When I Am 21

I'MAY NOT BE ABEL TO MAKE IT
21 BECASE OF WHAT I
REACT WHEN I'M OUT
THE STREET OR I
MOSTLY I'LL MAKE IT

I may not be able to make it (to) 21 because of what I react when I'm out (on) the street or mostly I'll make it

M

When I Am 21

When I am 21 I will be happy because I can look foward to alot of things like going to clubs, working, and living my own life. When you're young, you wish you could do more and when you hit 21, you become a real man. The thought of doing what you want is exciting to me and to many other kids. That's why I can't wait.

When I am 21 I will be happy because I can look forward to a lot of things like going to clubs, working, and living my own life. When you're young, you wish you could do more and when you hit 21, you become a real man. The thought of doing what you want is exciting to me and to many other kids. That's why I can't wait.

M 14-4

When I Am 21

I wish that when im 21, i will have a job, family, and friends. Because those are the Most important things in My life.

I wish that when I'm 21, I will have a job, family, and friends. Because those are the most important things in my life.

F 11-10

When I Am 21 I WAnt to
Sing

[assisted spelling: want sing]

I want to sing

M

When I Am 21
There is nothing for me
to write.

(assisted spelling: there nothing write)

There is nothing for me to write.

M 12-11

When I Am 21

Nothing

Nothing

F 14-2 When I Am 21

Nothing

Nothing

F 12-10

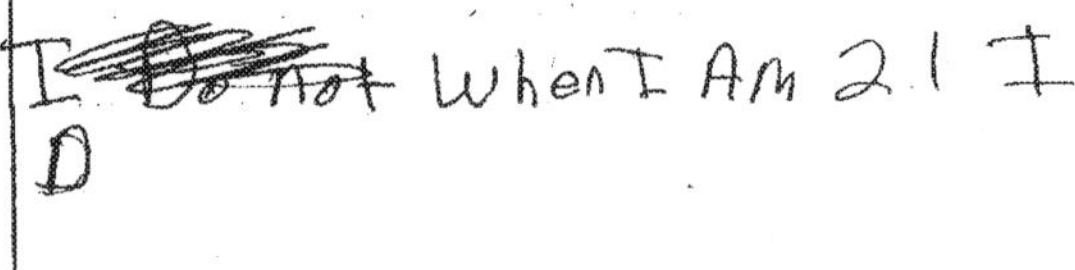
When I Am 21
I ~~Do not~~ When I Am 21 I
D
I Donot whish outhing.

[assisted spelling: wish]

I do not wish nothing.

M 13-4

When I Am 21

I don't wish nothing

I don't wish nothin

M 13-8

When I Am 21

I would go back in time ~~an~~ when I was 12 and get a second chance and I wont be her I wouldn't give my mom no trouble

I would go back in time (to) when I was 12 and get a second chance and I wouldn't be here I wouldn't give my mom no trouble

Abstract wishes: *Summary of Wishes*

a beautiful girlfriend
a fly girl with long black hair
a girl
a girl friend to keep me company
a healthy life
a lot of friends
a maid
a relationship with a female
a wealthy man
also the club scene no more getting-kicked out Im going to any club
And I will love to be 21 yrs old as a woman!!!
and last but not least I wish I can live in a world with-out violence, please excuse my spelling
And as I get older I hope I succeed in life so I could look back and say I acommplished something,
balanced budget
be a nice person
be able to travle
be all I can be
be brave and stand up for myself
be famous
be helthy and stay alive
be respected by my friends family and suroundings
be with my friends and family
buy clothes
by me close *(clothes)*
car losens *(car lessons - driving lessons)*
continue to collect comics
cute girl friend
depend on myself
Depending on the circumstances I would also like to start traveling during school brakes. Where I'm not sure but I would like to start,
do not want to be a bum or a drug attic
do the right thing
do thing I could not do when I was yound *(young)*
doing better for myself
dressing in $500 suits, dress suits'
Drinking license
everry thing I ask for

everyone will stop killing animals
friends
gang with friends
get me everthing i need
get out of forster care
get ticket to Purto Rico
girl
girl friend
go anywhere I want
go out every Friday night
go out somewhere with my friends
go places do things
go to another country
going to Alatanic City with my cousin timmy
Go to church
go to the casino gamble lucky number is 5,3.
good health
good healthy life
going to vacacion
great wisdom
hang out with my friends
hanggliding bunge jumping skiiing
happiness, good health, family and good friends
have a girl
have a girl friends
have a good life
have a happy life
have fun
have positive friends
hope to have all my goals for life accomplished. In other words I hope to have my life together
I also hope to stay away from trouble. I also hope trouble dose not find me
I also want to help kids with their self in how hard life is when you don't know your feelings and how you feel about thing. I also want to help the poor give money when I have, try and have a extra bathtube and up stairs in my house so they can shower I can give them something to eat and let them start fresh let them get a job and do the right them *(thing)* for themselves go back to school
I also wish not to end up back in the system
I am free at last
I am going to be happy
I am going to be old enough to drink and go to clubs.

I am gonna go to clubs. To tell you the truth I'm gonna have FUN!
I can do a lot of thing
I can do what I want to do so I don't have to listen to any one except myself!
I can drink beer
I can g *(go)* places
I do not got notting to whis for
I do not whish outhing *(nothing)*
I dont no *(know)*
I don't want to be in jail or any other thing either
I don't wish nothing
I hope also my exama *(eczema)* is gone
I hope I have a nice woman who love me and care for me the way I would care for her
I hope I live to get to 21.
I hope my life is to gether
I hope to accomplish my dream...
I hope to be happy and at peace with myself
I hope to be on my way to a succesful life
I hope to finish college
I hope to god that I will make the age 21.
I hope to have a girl friend.
I hope to have a good life
I hope to live a long happy life
I hope when Im 21 one I still look good to girl but better
I just wanna be succesful
I really like learning new things. I wanna be able to ieam and make money.
I may not be abel to make it *(to)* 21 because of what *(how)* I react when Im out the street
I might be on the road to a successful life or I might be on the road to "Hell".
I think first of all Im going to be able to drink whatever I want and also hang out as long as I want.
I think when Im 21 Im going to be happy but catious, because you can get into a lot of trouble.
I want to be the best I can as a basketball player and as a person.
I want to help kids to stop crime so we can show the people that always looked down at us.
I want black kids to have a better place to live. Instead of small tenements. So, in the 2000 century Blacks wouldn't be looked upon as the low lifes as now.
I want to be a nice young man and rely *(really)* well known

I want to be financially and mentally and phisically set
I want to be smart (get my edjucation) and get paid.
I want to be someone
I want to be successful and do something and not be a gangster
I want to be successful in life
I want to be with my boyfriend because we have a lot of plains for the future
I want to do things that I could not do as a child like go to part's *(parties)* for adults, and drive my own car
I want to get away from everything and everone
I want to get married to my girlfriend *(named)* and have two children (girl, boy)
I want to have a good life. I want to be happy.
I want to stay out of trouble mind my own buniss
I want to take dance classes so I can become a professional dancer in hip-hop
I wes *(wish)* I am alive
I will also help the homeless and the needy
I will be a man and noone will be my boss except the one at my job at the local hangout
I will be a role model
I will be able to buy beer
I will be famous
I will be happy
I will be happy because I can look forward to a lot of things like going to clubs, working, and living my own life
I will be old enough to do whatever I want
I will be rich and famaus
I will be someody
I will be the most "respected" man I the U.S.A
I will be 22 years old
I will have a great life
I will go out to a night club go back to my house and relax
I will go to clubs and have fun and stay out late.
I will have a good life and won't have to work any more me and my girl hopefulley my kids eather
I will have a happy life
I will help the needy
I will look back and laugh
I will make a difference
I will make something of myself

I will still be trying to enjoy life.
I will try to be a very responsible person.
I wish I can get an education and be somebody.
I wish I would get better and be more resposible.
I wish I would live to make pice, *(peace)*
I wish that I can make a contribution to this world but most of all I wish for my mother to get better from her disease.
I wish that I had a genie that would give me 3 wishes, that I would save my last wish
I wish that nobody in my family could not die and myself could not die
I wish the world will be a better place not only for myself but for my children and my family.
I wish to have all the beateful wemen
I wish to own the presedent
I wish when I am 21 I chold go to college.
I would buy anything I want that I wish for and thats it
I would do fun things in life.
I would ge my independents *(independence).*
I would go back in time...and get a second chance, good school for my kids, will like to be recanized throw out *(throughout) the* world as a heroick person!
I would go to any club, but before I do any thing I would by cigarettes with out no problem.
I would have a band on the side and I'd be the drummer, guitarist or bass guitarist.
I would like a tatoo on my chest
I would like to be already famous, and rich when I turn 21
I would like to be doing everything people said I couldn't do
I would like to be happy my oland tirr *(whole entire)* life so no one would brther *(bother)* me and my family
I would like to be my own self and speack for rights
I would like to be successful at everything I do.
I would like to do a lot of things. Things I haven't done yet. for example i want to go to parties, have my car, no children, and much freedom. The last thing is to have my boy friend pay the rent.
I would like to enjoy life by my self for awhile
I would like to start doing all the things I've not gotten around to in life, with my family or friends.
I would like to think I'll still have a girlfriend, as well as a personal and social life
I would like to travel all over the world in other words I would like to tour around the world with famous people like roll models.

I would love to feel the badge on my chest i love cops.
I would not depend on any one but my self.
I would not treat women bad because they brang us it to the world.
I would travel and explore new places that I have never seen before
I would want to just start over of my life
I would wish for nothing
I would wish to go home.
I would wish to keep the fame that I get when I turned 18
I wouldn't be someone that smokes & drinks just because I am of age to
I'll be able to drink and go to clubs
I'll be able to get into rated R movies
I'll be able to move out of my house
I'll be working and when I come home I'll be playing as many game as I want!
I'm just a simple person who wants simple things, and hopefully I'll be able to get what I want out of life now and when I get older
I'm not focus on what I'm gonna do when I'm twenty-one, because I'm only fourteen and I'm focusing on what's going on in my life now like going home, and starting my life over.
I'm not sure,
if I make it to 21
If I was 21 years old I would be going ever where I want
independent individual with a good job
It will be the life
it's better to change when ur young than to wait until it's to late.
Jahovah
learn more about myself, do not make the same mistakes I made in my past
learn to fight for myself
live ahappy life
live by myself
live happy for the rest of my life
live on my own
live with a dog name Doughboy
live with one dog
living on my own
long way til 21 hopefully I will make it
love and happiness
mainly relax during summers
Make love

make my own decisions
make something of myself
my body will be in shape
my driver's license
my girl friend will like who I am
no criminal record
no wars
Nobody hate me everybody love me I don't hate I love to *(too)*
nothing
Nothing
On Tuesdays and Thursdays I will read and listen to poetry at small Bohemian night clubs, were eventually I will meet the man of my dreams. He will move into my spacius loft apartment which is conviently located right around the corner, and we'll live happily ever after
own my own school
party all night
play drums better
play Nintindo 64
powers
providing family and friends with anything they need
raise a dog
see my girl friend
smoking cigarettes
so when my life is all straighten up, I'll be so happy that nothing could make me depress again
someone to care for
spend more time with my family and friends
steady girlfriend
still go to church
still have family and friends
talk to my cottage mates
that everyone would have homes to go to
that there will be no more violence in the world
The only thing that I wish for, is to be alive and happy. To me, nothing is more important over then being here on earth. There a lot of great things on earth and a lot that I would like to achieve. So I wish for life and true happiness
Then maybe thing would be much more easyer then benning *(being) 13.* Having a life that is not so perfect I can say 13 was a hard year for me having problem I never had in the other year!
there is nothing for me to write.
to be a good basketball player

to be able to take care of myself and my home

to be happy all the time

to be healthy and happy

to be in shape

to be on my own

to drive a car

To find my birth mother

to fly

to go on a talk show and find my lost girlfriend who moved to Washinton. I wish for this 'cause I loved her with all my heart and when she left I couldn't say good-bye

to have privacy

to just live to make it through life

to know Michael Jackson

to still be alive

to still pray

to stop being to my girl on all kinds of ways most of the time I wish that we be there for each other for life

try not to fight

very nice life

Want to be happy and my girl happy to

want to be in good health

want to be in shape at 21 so I could feel strong untill I get older

Want to become famous

Want to do whatever I want

want to meet Micheal Jordan in real life and I want to play against Micheal Jordan to see who is the best in basketball

want to stay away from trouble

Well I wouldn't say anything that wont come true

whant don't no body in my car when Im not ther except my wife and borthe *(brother)*

What I want is to live a straight life. To live sivil

When I am 21 all I wish for in a nutshell is happiness, good health, family and good friends

What I mean by having a life is getting my shelf together and be very smart. To love and care for another, but in order to do so, I must love my shelf first to love anybody else

when I am 21 I am free

When I am 21 I want to be able to have the knowledge and know how to be on my own, and have a well-paying job so I could support myself without anyones help

When I am 21 I want to be able to say that my childhood and teenage hood didn't go to waste. I want to be able to say I had fun with my friends, and finished high school (at least) at the same time

When I'am 21 I going to go out to a club have a couple of drinks and party and no one can say anything about it cause I'am 21 an adult!

When I am 21 I hope to have all my goals for my life accomplished. In other words I hope to have my life together. Some examples of these things are having a car, being well along in my college and having a good job. I also hope by then I can spend more time with my family and friends.

When I reach that age I still want to be alive

When I'm 21 years old, I would want to just start over of my life

will be a role model

will be famous

will be somebody

will help the needy

will listen

will live a good life

will make a difference

will make something of myself

Will never smoke or drink I will be very healthy

win the lotto

wish I am alive

with a good head on my shoulders

with all posotive friends

would also like to take a vacation to Germany or Ireland

would help younger children to read

would like to have a good life

Would like to see more peace on heart *(earth)*

Would like to travel all over the world

Would not like to be a couch potato, would like to be physically active

would want to just start over of my life

Abstract Wishes: *Commentary*

I find most noteworthy those wishes that refer to personal virtues ('be brave', 'will listen', 'to still pray') and those that refer to a world outside of and bigger than ourselves (16) ('a world without violence', 'peace on earth', 'help younger children to read', 'everyone will stop killing animals', 'will help the needy').

A discussion of goals for improving spiritual health could lead to topics such as values and virtues, and our need and desire to connect with the bigger world. Again, we can choose particular goals and work with the student to formulate sub-goals suitable for the present time. For instance, one student has a goal of giving food at Christmas to the needy. We can assist the student in making this a reality by identifying a location willing to accept food (local food kitchen perhaps), and devising a plan to have students and members of the school community donate food or money. We assist the student in listing the myriad details, such as permission from the principal, announcing our plan to the school, specifying the foods suitable for donation, and arranging transportation to the recipient organization. (21)

Happiness as a concept can be explored and more specifically defined, especially as it relates to students' current lives.

Concrete wishes: *Student Papers*

M 9-4

When I Am 21

Dog fish Hamster.

(Assisted spelling: hamster)

dog fish hamster

M

When I Am 21

I would like a Dog or a cat
I would like a good Job
and a faimle

I would like a dog or a cat I would like a good job and a family

F 16-6

When I Am 21

~~When~~

When I turn 21 I hope I have a bank account because at that age the agency kicks you out and if I don't have no money I won't have nowhere to live.

When I turn 21 I hope I have a bank account because at that age the agency kicks you out and if I don't have no money I won't have nowhere to live.

Concrete wishes: *Summary of Wishes*

a bank account
a boat
a book
a dog or a cat
a license to drive
a lot of credit cards; and money
a lot of dogs
a lot of video games
a map
a 100 disease Riden ladys, *(disease-ridden ladies)*
all the toys in the world
basketball hoop in my house
can own building
cats
dirtbike
dog
dog fish hamster
dog of my own
dogs
driveway
food
fun funture *(furniture)*
good things
glock 7 for protection
have a phone
have a pond whit fish in it so I can fish in the pond
have my own compeuter
have the best clothes in the world
hope to have nice things and good hair
I will buy a lot of 40 oz beer
I will have 2 dogs
I will wont a sketor *(skater)*
I would like to have a boy beagle dog; to keep me from being lonely and have my spirit high
I would wish for a cake and ice camme *(cream)* for my brithday. and to see my sister and my couin *(cousin).*
lots of video games
lots of pets
montin bike

name brad cloth *(name brand clothes)* and coats a *(and)* snekers
new clothes
new sneakers
pool
pool indoor and outdoor
shoes
sneakers
some clothes and sneaker
store
very very big DJ
would buy extremely expensive clothes and jewelry not fake, I'm talking about some real diamonds and gold here

Concrete wishes: *Commentary*

As with cars and homes, we can distinguish between fantasies ('outdoor pool') and more realistic possibilities ('book', 'furniture').

Wishes for pets are poignant and tap into basic human needs for nurturance and companionship. I believe that animals are therapeutic and have an important place in the school community and environment. Students should learn how to care for animals as part of the spiritual health curriculum.

The same guidelines discussed with money issues apply here, namely, what is the cost of the desired item and how does this cost fit into our budget?

Chapter Two: Social Goals

Introduction: Social Skills

In talking with our students about their problems, for instance why they are in residential placement, I have found it useful to speak of their 'difficulties with social skills'. By social skills we are referring to the entire range of social and personal relations, including peers, family members, teammates, classmates, adult staff and employers. 'Having difficulties with social skills' is much less threatening than 'emotionally disturbed' and more accurately communicates what we want to say and what we want the students to see as a healthful path to their growth and to their future. We want the students to address their present difficulties by creating a plan involving specific actions. We do not want them to focus on 'emotional disturbances' experienced prior to placement and continuing up to the present.

Most students will agree that they have problems getting along with others, for instance with anger management, and with controlling their aggressive impulses. We do not seek the 'why'; we seek the 'what are we going to do about it?' Discussing emotions leads our students inward, where they are vulnerable and defensive. 'Social skills' points them outward, towards others, where we can focus on our words and on our communication skills. Students may have learned that discussing their past brings them sympathy and attention, but I don't see that this is helpful in moving forward. The exception is when the student himself brings up his past, and an opportunity thereby presents itself for a meaningful intervention, or for being a good listener.

We focus on the current state of their personal relationships, and how we can improve them. We are now the adults in their lives, serving *in loco parentis.* If students are sincere about improving their social skills, we will have ample opportunity to see firsthand, in how they relate to us and to others.

Group work provides an excellent forum for working on social skills. We use the already established student groups. (23) Speaking and listening skills are the intersection of social skills with language skills. (24) The improvement of communication skills, with language and vocabulary development, tone of voice, eye contact and body language directly address social skills. We teach students alternate ways of speaking, different words that have more precise connotations, naming adjectives more descriptive than 'good' wife, 'nice' family and 'good' children. Students learn to use new words to describe their experiences and their wishes. They also learn to name personal characteristics, virtues and values of people (including themselves), who are important in their lives. The student group provides the forum to practice these skills.

Adult relations: *Student Papers*

F

Adult Relations

What are my goals for improving my skills with adult relations?

By not disrespecting them If I fell wrong I their Just don't say anything I Just say yes and walk away I fell that If you dont disrespect you probably will get the respect you dezerve So I don't disrespect anyone anymore my saying I say when I'm mad

You Have To give Respect To Get Respect

By not disrespecting them If I (feel) (they're) wrong I just don't say anything I just say yes and walk away. I (feel) that if you don't disrespect you probably will get the respect you deserve so I don't disrespect anyone anymore my saying I say when I'm mad

You Have To give Respect To Get Respect

F

Adult Relations

What are my goals for improving my skills with adult relations?

I need to stop rolling my eyes at people and sucking my teeth. Oh yeah and stop getting smart and follow instructions Plus I need stop cursing at my autority figures.

I need to stop roiling my eyes at people and sucking my teeth. Oh yeah and stop getting smart and follow instructions. Plus I need to stop cursing at my authority figures.

(Unknown)

Adult Relations

What are my goals for improving my skills with adult relations?

I should ~~mak~~. listen before I talk. Maybe if I listen my life could be so. much better not only with Adults but kids too.

I should listen before I talk. Maybe If I listen my life could be so much better not only with adults but kids too.

(Page 1 of 2)

(Unknown)

Adult Relations

What are my goals for improving my skills with adult relations?

I think that I get annoyed easily when adults ask me questions. And sometim if they ask me too many I just say "I don't know". I mean I really do know but I just don't want to talk and that makes them mad. But I still do it anyway. I seem to have a hard time explaining myself to adults. At school I always have an attitude with my teachers. And when I do have an attitude sometimes I feel bad because they don't always have an attitude towards me. except my math teacher

(Page 2 of 2)

I think that I get annoyed easily when adults ask me questions. And sometimes if they ask me too many I just say "I don't know". I mean I really do know but I just don't want to talk and that makes them mad. But I still do it anyway. I seem to have a hard time explaining myself to adults. At school I always have an attitude with my teachers. And when I do have an attitude sometimes I feel bad because they don't always have an attitude towards me except my math teacher (teacher's name).

F

Adult Relations

What are my goals for improving my skills with adult relations?

I wonna be able to egnor. I wonna be able not to Assume. I wonna be able to not get agitated, But some times you just are having a bad day. I hope to ready for anything. I also wonna know what the topic is befor we start to talk cause, I wonna be able to handle it or say I do not wonna talk about it. Some times they make ~~you~~ me and that just makes me mad. I already can have a conversation with adults fine. When I'm up set like when any one else with my life would proble react More harshly or more ~~better~~ beter I react my own way. Some times I am quiet and and Say please leave me alone. or I do not wonna talk or hear about that, But they keep on and that makes me up set.

(Page 2 of 2)

I wanna be able to ignore. I wanna be able not to assume. I wanna be able to not get agitated, But sometimes you just are having a bad day. I hope to (be) ready for anything. I also wanna know what the topic is before we start to talk cause I wanna be able to handle it or say I do not wanna talk about it. Sometimes they make me and that just makes me mad. I already can have a conversation with adults fine. When I'm upset like when any else with my life would probably react more harshly or more bitter I react my own way. Sometimes I am quiet and say please leave me alone or I do not wanna talk or hear about that. But they keep on and that makes me upset.

M

What are my goals for improving my skills with adult relations? I would Focus on how my lannage is around adults

I would focus on how my language is around adults

(Unknown)

Adult Relations

What are my goals for improving my skills with adult relations?

I will take an anger manigmint class.

I will take an anger management class.

Adult Relations

F

What are my goals for improving my skills with adult relations?

I want to improve my listening skills with adults.

I want to improve my listening skills with adults.

(Unknown)

Adult Relations

What are my goals for improving my skills with adult relations?

I what to stop fighting watn Adults.

I want to stop fighting with adults.

(Unknown)

Adult Relations

What are my goals for improving my skills with adult relations? man I know know this is a stupid question improving skills for adult relations I don't believe in that and I don't need to I get along with everybody.

man I know now this is a stupid question improving skills for adult relations I don't believe in that and I don't need to get along with everybody.

M

Adult Relations

What are my goals for improving my skills with adult relations?

My goal would be to stop cursing at adults when I'm talking to them.

My goal would be to stop cursing at adults when I'm talking to them.

M

Adult Relations

What are my goals for improving my skills with adult relations?

my goals for improving my Skills in Adult Relations are to listen and agree with Adult Points also to be more open minded and More mature.

My goals for improving my skills in Adult Relations are to listen and agree with Adult points also to be more open minded and more mature

F

Adult Relations

What are my goals for improving my skills with adult relations?

My goals for improving my skills with adult relations is that if they respect me, I will respect them right back. Also I have to improve my additue with adult. Because Sometime I could just Come out with an additue, and don't mean it. But I'm Working on that. Also I have to follow Adult rules. Cauze Sometimes I break the rules and do what I want to do. But that's going to change in order for me to go back home.

My goals for improving my skills with adult relations is that if they respect me, I will respect them right back. Also I have to improve my attitude with adults. Because sometime I could just come out with an attitude, and don't mean it. But I'm working on that. Also I have to follow Adult rules, cause sometimes I break the rules and do what I want to do. But that's going to change in order for me to go back home.

F

Adult Relations

What are my goals for improving my skills with adult relations? My goals for improving my skills with adult relations is to stop cursing at adult's an stop hiting adults too.

My goals for improving my skills with adult relations is to stop cursing at adults and stop hitting adults too.

F

Adult Relations

What are my goals for improving my skills with adult relations?

My goals for improving my skills with adult Relations, are I want to be more respectful. Listen to older peoples directions. And work on me and my mothers relationship.

My goals for improving my skills with adult relations, are I want to be more respectful. Listen to older people's directions. And work on me and my mother's relationship.

F

Adult Relations

What are my goals for improving my skills with adult relations?

My goals is toget along ~~with~~ with adult
And stop hitting on the Staff

My goals is to get along with adults And stop hitting on the staff

M

Adult Relations

What are my goals for improving my skills with adult relations?

My relations with adults are satisfactory except for my temper and my ability to analyze everything. I hope to keep both under control when dealing with adults

My relations with adults are satisfactory except for my temper and my ability to analyze everything. I hope to keep both under control when dealing with adults

F

Adult Relations

What are my goals for improving my skills with adult relations?

My relationship with adults on my block are not very good., I dont really get along with them, But I do hang out With there children. I think I can talk to the parents one on one to Show them Im not a bad Person, And im worthy of hangout with there daughtors/son's.

My relationship with adults on my block are not very good. I don't really get along with them, But I do hang out with their children. I think I can talk to the parents one on one to show them I'm not a bad person And I'm worthy of hang(ing) out with their daughters/sons.

M (Page 1 of 2)

Adult Relations

What are my goals for improving my skills with adult relations?

No screaming at adult
and respect your elders
don't fight with adult
You respect adult at all times
No talking back to adult

don't try to get smart and
break one of there stuff
when your mad gust talk it
out all the time be nice
and cool and respect your elders

(Page 2 of 2)

No screaming at adults and respect your elders
don't fight with adult(s)
You respect adult(s) at all times
No talking back to adult(s)
don't try to get smart and break one of their stuff
When you're mad just talk it out all the time be nice and cool and respect your elders

M (Page 1 of 2)

Adult Relations

What are my goals for improving my skills with adult relations?

1) Talkout Problens and make it better

2) Show respect and give kindness, listen

3) admit that you are wrong at times

4) Just be yourself, and do all of the above.

(Page 2 of 2)

1) Talk out problems and make it better

2) Show respect and give kindness; listen

3) admit that you are wrong at times

4) Just be yourself and do all of the above

(Unknown)

Adult Relations

What are my goals for improving my skills with adult relations?

The ways That I can improve my'skills is to Look a adult in the eye, and to Be more mature when I am around a adult.

The ways that I can improve my skills is to look a(n) adult in the eye, and to be more mature when I am around a(n) adult.

F

Adult Relations

What are my goals for improving my skills with adult relations? To become more trust worthy with them, To let myself trust them more, To get to know them, To get it throught my head that they ain't all the Same

To become more trustworthy with them, To let myself trust them more, To get to know them, To get it through my head that they ain't all the same.

Adult relations: *Commentary*

Regarding adult relations, we can begin to generate discussion by asking students in a non-threatening way to talk about the qualities they would like certain adults in their lives to have, for instance, athletic coach, teacher, principal, tutor, parents. (23) If appropriate, students could discuss disappointments with various adults currently or previously in their lives. Qualities that students would like to see in adults generally reflect how they themselves would like to be treated by adults. As students specify and detail exactly how they would like to be treated - under a variety of social circumstances - they are using and developing vocabulary and language skills. This in turn opens the door to how we should treat others, namely, as we ourselves would like to be treated. (24) We take their stated goals for improving their adult relations and we work individually with students to devise specific steps and sub-goals.

Staff who work with our youngsters need to be aware of both positive and, especially, negative transference. Briefly, transference is the carrying over of emotions, images and ideas from one adult to another. Transference is a defense mechanism; in the act of protecting himself, the student generalizes the new adult by believing that the new adult has many of the same characteristics as previous adults and by acting toward the new adult in a way similar to how he acted toward the previous adult. We all do this to some extent. We couldn't survive if we didn't generalize (27). Problems with abused and neglected students often arise when students transfer onto staff negative and angry feelings carried over from previous adult/authority figures. It is emotionally challenging for staff to bear the heat of these negative feelings; herein lies our work, however, namely for staff not to respond with anger, and for the student to learn that not all adults are the same, and that authority figures can be kind, patient and nurturing. In this way, staff can break the transference and allow the student to see more clearly who is who, who treated him badly and who is treating him respectfully. This in turn allows the student to have more satisfying relations with adults as each adult is seen and treated as an individual - a goal surely the student has for herself.

Peer relations: *Student Papers*

F

Peer Relations

What are my goals for improving my skills with peer relations?

the Same as an adult. If they respect me, I will give the Same respect right back. But If they come to me on Some Stupid shit, than I got to put them on check. But other than that I could be cool with my peer.

The same as an adult. If they respect me, I will give the same respect right back. But if they come to me on some stupid shit, then I got to put them on check. But other than that I could be cool with my peer(s).

F

Peer Relations

What are my goals for improving my skills with peer relations?

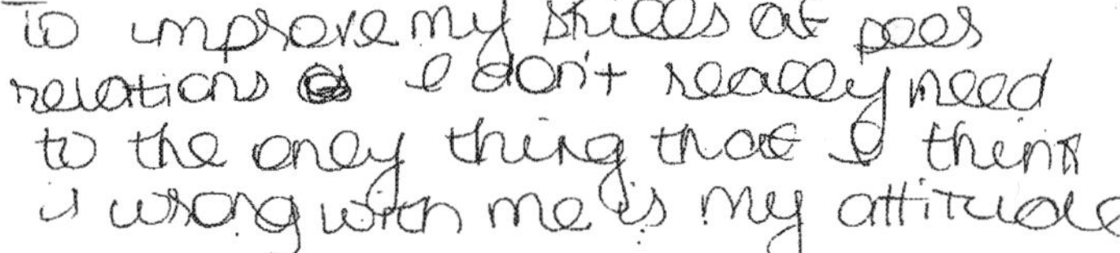

To improve my skills of peer relations I don't really need to the only thing that I think is wrong with me is my attitude

F

Peer Relations

What are my goals for improving my skills with peer relations?

Well I don't really have goals to improve my relations with my Peers because I Came here by myself and I'm leaving by myself and if Someone does not like me that's on them.

Well I don't really have goals to Improve my relations with my peers because I came here by myself and I'm leaving by myself and if someone does not like me that's on them.

F

Peer Relations

What are my goals for improving my skills with peer relations?

My relationship with my friends are
pretty good, I think im very friendly and very
easy going. I make friends fast.
Sometime I make hang out with the
wrong group or kids and end up doing something
that could get me into trouble, But later
on I learn from my mistakes.

My relationship with my friends are pretty good. I think I'm very friendly and very easy going. I make friends fast. Sometime(s) I (may) hang out with the wrong group of kids and end up doing something that could get me into trouble, But later on I learn from my mistakes.

F

Peer Relations

What are my goals for improving my skills with peer relations?

One problem that I really have is like I'm really talkative and sometimes I run my mouth so much it gets me into problems. Sometimes I get into problems that have nothing to do with me. Like these girls from Flushing wanted to jump [illegible]. Like [illegible] is not really a good friend and I fought two of them and I cut one with a razor thing and I almost got arrested because I dropped the razor and when they searched me I didnt have it. Now if I got charged that would have been terrible.

One problem that I really have is like I'm really talkative and sometimes I run my mouth so much it gets me into problems. Sometimes I get into problems that have nothing to do with me. Like these girls from Flushing wanted to jump (girl's name). Like (girl's name) is not really a good friend and I fought two of them and I cut one with a razor thing and I almost got arrested because I dropped the razor and when they searched me I didn't have it. Now if I got charged that would have been terrible.

(Unknown)

Peer Relations

What are my goals for improving my skills with peer relations?

Maybe if I Stop using, my fist ant sometime use my mouth life would be much better,

Maybe if I stop using my fist and sometime use my mouth life would be much better.

F

Peer Relations

What are my goals for improving my skills with peer relations?

My goals for improving my skills with peer relations is to be me not some phoney chick who just want to fit in the crowded. What I'm saying is if you don't like what I bring to the table then don't take it.

My goals for improving my skills with peer relations is to be me not some phony chick who just want to fit in (with) the (crowd). What I'm saying is if you don't like what I bring to the table then don't take it.

M

Peer Relations

What are my goals for improving my skills with peer relations?

If I had any true peers I would be open Minded and listen to what they have to say, I would also be totally honest with them and last But not least. I would try and Solve any conflicts they or we may have.

If I had any true peers I would be open minded and listen to what they have to say, I would also be totally honest with them and last but not least I would try and solve any conflicts they or we may have.

F

Peer Relations

What are my goals for improving my skills with peer relations?

Just to egnore Negatice things when your Peer's say thing's you dont like Just walk away or say I dont like the way you talk to me but say it Respectful so they wont come at you wrong so you and that person wont have any problem's. Don't be a butt kisser but that's what you have to be sometimes for peice especially If you live together that's the best policy.

Just to ignore negative things when your peers say things you don't like Just walk away or say I don't like the way you talk to me but say it respectful so they won't come at you wrong so you and that person won't have any problems. Don't be a butt kisser but that's what you have to be sometimes for peace especially if you live together that's the best policy.

M

Peer Relations

What are my goals for improving my skills with peer relations?

I probaly need to learn to socalize better because I don't like to talk. And I like anything or anybody who doesn't talk.

I probably need to learn to socialize better because I don't like to talk. And I like anything or anybody that doesn't talk.

F

Peer Relations

What are my goals for improving my skills with peer relations?

I want to stay to myself a little so I don't get into trouble and get into gossip and problems so I can avoid problems, And not touch nobody elses stuff. And don't get into problem.

I want to stay to myself a little so I don't get into trouble and get into gossip and problems so I can avoid problems, And not touch nobody else's stuff. And don't get into problem(s).

M

Peer Relations

What are my goals for improving my skills with peer relations?

I dont really have problem with peer relation. Im going to try to stop fighting.

I don't really have (a) problem with peer relation(s). Im going to try to stop fighting.

F

Peer Relations

What are my goals for improving my skills with peer relations?

I have an anger problem and I need to know how to solve problems verbally and not physically. I also have a problem with trusting tomany people.

I have an anger problem and I need to know how to solve problems verbally and not physically. I also have a problem with trusting (too) many people.

(Unknown)

Peer Relations

What are my goals for improving my skills with peer relations?

1) egnore
2) walk away
3) talk to staff
4) Deep Breathing
5 count 1-10

1) ignore
2) walk away
3) talk to staff
4) deep breathing
5) count 1-10

(Unknown)

Peer Relations

What are my goals for improving my skills with peer relations?

I can stop cursing and Learn how to control my Thoughts as well.

I can stop cursing and learn how to control my thoughts as well.

M (Page 1 of 2)

Peer Relations

What are my goals for improving my skills with peer relations?

1) don't judge people's character hurtfully

2) Hear their side of the story; then tell mine and then go over them

3) Give important advice, (if needed)

4) be yourself at all times

(Page 2 of 2)

1) don't judge people's character hurtfully

2) Hear their side of the story; then tell mine and then go over them

3) Give important advice, (if needed).

4) be yourself at all times

M

Essay = How can I improve in getting along with my peers.

By talk good to peers. By teaching them how to do something that they don't know how to do like, basketball, math or reading. By talking about how they feel about coming here. Teach them about their religon. By talking about how they feel a person. Asking how they feel today. How did they feel at they home vist. By not saying things that they don't want to hear.

By talk(ing) good to peers. By teaching them how to do something that they don't know how to do like, basketball, math or reading. By talking about how they feel about coming here. Teach them about their religion. By talking about how they feel (as) a person. Asking how they feel today. How did they feel at (their) home visit. By not saying things that they don't want to hear.

(Unknown)

Peer Relations

What are my goals for improving my skills with peer relations?

Well my goal for improving my skills with peer relations is to calm my attitude down, also not to pay attention to negative people who come around. I also will try not to pay attention to gossip.

Well my goal for improving my skills with peer relations is to calm my attitude down, also not to pay attention to negative people who come around. I also will try not to pay attention to gossip.

Peer relations: *Commentary*

Peer relations are generally the greatest single indicator both of social/emotional health and happiness/sadness for individuals throughout society. (28) Peer relations is the arena wherein questions of autonomy, maturity, morality, virtue and interpersonal satisfaction come together. Love interests encompass the spiritual, the emotional and the physical. We examine students' current wishes for improving their social skills with peers and, if need be, we can return to **Chapter 1** (Family) and revisit their wishes for a spouse. In this way we can - with certain students - bring together wishes for a spouse with current goals for improving peer relationships. When the student is comfortable and articulate with his goals, we are in a position to establish sub-goals.

The mature individual recognizes that success and the attainment of money and material goods are of value only to the extent that we can enjoy sharing them with others.

Teenagers are forming their identity, and conflicts between autonomy and group identity are often troublesome. These conflicts bear directly on student goals and may present obstacles to their attainment. The peer group dynamic is very strong, as is group identity. Pressure to conform to the mores of the group can be exceedingly high. The positive aspect of the peer group is that the individual seeks to connect with a larger world, an aspect of human nature that hopefully will find positive fruition, for instance in his work, in his family and/or in his citizenship.

The extent to which the individual can rise to her/his own level of autonomy and virtue will often be a central determinate in that person's quest for satisfying peer relations, as well as for personal happiness and fulfillment. This process directly addresses a student's strength of autonomy and sense of morality. Regarding autonomy, there are many factors in the student's maturation process that affect the development of a strong sense of self and self-confidence. Regarding morality, for students in residential placement, who generally have lacked strong parental moral modeling and guidance, it is often (though not always) necessary for them to get this sense of morality elsewhere, presumably/hopefully from an adult(s) serving *in loco parentis.* Some few individuals, from strength of character, are able to attain strong moral principles without the guidance and/or modeling of an adult. This strength, or lack thereof, is tested or borne out as one decides when to be a part of the peer group, and when to be independent from the peer group. One can be a part of a peer group and not necessarily endorse every value of the group, just as one can be a member of a political party or religious denomination and not necessarily endorse the lot of beliefs that the party or religion endorses.

The peer group binds its members into a social unit with a common set of values and beliefs. The group functions to maintain and protect itself and its identity, and the mature individual sees where and when to be a part of the group and where and when to be an individual apart from the group. The real issues here are of confidence in oneself, security with one's opinions and one's character, and having the courage and morality to look within oneself to decide how to act in a particular situation. (28)

Group dynamics with our students involving guided discussion with already established school groups (23) can be a very effective way to value autonomy and independent thinking, to reveal - and in many cases to dispel - some of the unspoken values generally associated with student peer groups. For instance, and these examples are from my own experience, one of the assumed values of teens is that physical strength and sexual experience are highly valued. This is part of street lore, the set of street values common to inner-city youths. However, when youngsters, in the context of student groups, are asked to 'name three qualities that you would want in a potential boyfriend/girlfriend' these values are not mentioned. What is mentioned is the wish to be treated and respected as an individual; and when we tease out what is meant by respect, we get qualities such as being a good listener, paying attention, caring about what makes the person unique, speaking politely, being loyal. Here we have the opportunity to encourage respectful conversation and to develop a more mature vocabulary as we name characteristics that we seek and are attracted to in others, as well as attributes that we wish for ourselves.

(Unknown)

Character

What are my goals for improving my character?

By Being polite and generous considerate and sympathetic.

by being polite and generous considerate and sympathetic

(Unknown)

Character

What are my goals for improving my character? - Stop being so argumentive and arrogant towards my family.

stop being so argumentative and arrogant towards my family

F

Character

What are my goals for improving my character?

change my attitude and Smile more often

change my attitude and smile more often

F

Character

What are my goals for improving my character?

I have some problem controlling my actions. When people say stuff about me I lose my temper. Sometimes I let people get the best of me. I would like to controll my tempe and don't let people walk all over me. I got to learn how to turn my back on wrong an look write in the face. and say I have found you at last

I have some problem controlling my actions. When people say stuff about me I lose my temper. Sometimes I let people get the best of me. I would like to control my temper and don't let people walk all over me. I got to learn how to turn my back on wrong and look right in the face, and say I have found you at last

F

Character

What are my goals for improving my character?

I have. this therapist named and
e tells me that I have a lot of anger inside
nd I take it out on the wrong people. I think
at's true. Mabye I do take it out on the
rong people also I'm very easily persuaded
my peers. Like to do bad things like one
ime my best friend was having
hookie party and I was not going to
o but she talked me into it. I try try.
ry to be nice. If youre nice to me I
ould be as sweet as sugar. But sometimes
irls especially have these attitude problems
nd. I don't like to fight but girls start
o much and when I fight I just blank out
nd thats not good so I tried hard for
months not to have no fights so far
o good.

(Page 2 of 2)

I have this therapist named (name) and she tells me that I have a lot of anger inside and I take it out on the wrong people. I think that's true. Maybe I do take it out on the wrong people also I'm very easily persuaded by my peers. Like to do bad things like one time my best friend (name) was having a nookie party and I was not going to go but she talked me into it. I try try try to be nice. If you're nice to me I could be as sweet as sugar. But sometimes girls especially have these attitude problems and I don't like to fight but girls start too much and when I fight I just blank out and that's not good so I tried hard for 2 months not to have no fights so far so good.

(Unknown)

Character

What are my goals for improving my character?

I need to stop being boring and just be happy! :)

I need to stop being boring and just be happy!

(Unknown)

Character

What are my goals for improving my character?

I will not be someone elis and I will be my self.

I will not be someone else and I will be myself.

(Unknown)

Character

What are my goals for improving my character?

Loose my attitude. Choose friends wisely.

Lose my attitude. Choose friends wisely.

F

Character

What are my goals for improving my character?

Just to be nice to others avoid problems and Just Stay tomyself and don't say everyones my friend I have a habit of that everyones not my friend theer my associates. So what I need to improve is stop calling everyone my friend.

Just to be nice to others
avoid problems and just stay to myself and don't say everyone's my friend I have a habit of that everyone's not my friend they're my associates, so what I need to improve is stop calling everyone my friend.

F (Page 1 of 2)

Character

What are my goals for improving my character?

~~my ch~~

My character is a funny yet confussed and frustrated person. My charector is nice. I feel I should have not been through or should not be going through some of the things I am going through. I feel I had and have my head on right but I ~~am~~ am having it pulled of ~~by~~ problems. I wish all my problems could go away. I wish I was home with mom we have money. my family comes over we go there. ~~xxx~~ I hope my Exema goes away ~~that~~ I grow out of it. I also hope to be able to be thin with beautiful hair with no split ends. I hope to stay in school finish go get a great Job. I hope to be less frustrated. But with all the problems how can I be not frustrated and mad.

(Page 2 of 2)

My character is a funny yet confused and frustrated person. My character is nice. I feel I should have not been through or should not be going through some of the things I am going through. I feel I had and have my head on right but I am having it pulled off by problems. I wish all my problems could go away. I wish I was home with mom we have money my family comes over we go there. I hope my eczema goes away that I grow out of it. I also hope to be able to be there with beautiful hair with no split ends. I hope to stay in school finish go get a great job. I hope to be less frustrated. But with all the problems how can I be not frustrated and mad.

F

Character

What are my goals for improving my character?

my tone of voice
coping skills

my tone of voice
coping skills

(Unknown)

Character

What are my goals for improving my character?

To act like the real me.

To act like the real me.

F

Character

What are my goals for improving my character?

To stop cursing, rolling my eyes, sucking my teeth, and actin
out of character.

To stop cursing, rolling my eyes, sucking my teeth, and acting out of character.

F

Character

What are my goals for improving my character?

Well my goals are to improving my character is to be more polite to people. Be more friendly, more open, and change my additue.

Well my goals to improving my character is to be more polite to people. Be more friendly, more open, and change my attitude.

M

Character

What are my goals for improving my character? Speak Polite to people Defend the one love.

Speak Polite to people and to Defend the ones that I love if they have Problems with money, fighting, and if they need to talk.

Speak polite to people and to defend the ones that I love if they have problems with money, fighting, and if they need to talk.

(Unknown)

Character

What are my goals for improving my character?

My goal for improving my character are to be more thoughtfull and open.

My goal for improving my character are to be more thoughtful and open.

(Unknown)

Character

What are my goals for improving my character?

Well my goal to improving myself is to keep focus on school and do the best I can. I can also improve myself by keeping cool and do not be so eager because in time everything will come.

Well my goal to improving myself is to keep focus on school and do the best I can. I can also improve myself by keeping cool and do not be so eager because in time everything will come.

M

Character

What are my goals for improving my character?

My goals for Improving My Character are: To try and mature as quickly as possible to try and Control my anger and turn a Neg. (-) in to a pos. (+)

To be more responcable.

My goals for improving my character are:

to try and mature as quickly as possible

to try and control my anger and turn a negative into a positive

to be more responsible.

Character: *Commentary*

The first item I wish to discuss here is the inclusion of the topic of character under the umbrella of social skills. It can be argued (and I think, correctly) that character is defined by the totality of one's values and virtues, as manifest in the person's actions, not only in relation to others but also in relation to oneself and to worlds beyond our immediate social spheres. For instance, one may value perseverance as a personal virtue, associated with dedication to task and application of discipline. In this context, perseverance is a personal goal bearing on one's relationship to oneself, outside the realm of social context. However, I do include character under the social umbrella with our specific population of students since so much of their pathology is manifest in their personal relations. In discussing character It is interesting to notice which comments students mention that relate to oneself, that relate to other persons, and that relate to larger worlds beyond our circle of family and friends.

I often had to explain to students what is meant by 'character'. However, once students heard the explanation, they had no difficulty in communicating their goals on the subject. I defined character as the sum of one's virtues, vices and values, as manifest in one's actions. I defined virtues, with examples, as qualities generally (if not totally) consistent with what most people would describe as 'good' or positive, and vices as qualities most people would describe as 'bad' or negative. Values, on the other hand, are defined as what one considers important in his/her life.

It is here that we get to flesh out students' desires for autonomy and definition. How do we see ourselves? What characteristics would we use to describe ourselves? How do we wish to improve our lives? What virtues do we seek for ourselves?

Watch your thoughts:
They become your words.
Watch your words:
They become your actions.
Watch your actions:
They become your habits.
Watch your habits:
They become your character.
Watch your character:
It becomes your destiny. (29)

Citizenship: *Student Papers*

(Unknown)

Citizenship

What are my goals for improving my citizenship?

To be more helpful towards my neighbors.

To be more helpful towards my neighbors.

M

Citizenship

What are my goals for improving my citizenship?

~~Helping old people~~ on christmas give people food

On Christmas give people food

M

Citizenship

What are my goals for improving my citizenship?

I really don't care about citizenship, and I don't pay it any attention.

I really don't care about citizenship and I don't pay it any attention.

(Unknown)

Citizenship

What are my goals for improving my citizenship?

by helping moor by being a positive Role model

by helping more by being a positive role model

(Unknown)

Citizenship

What are my goals for improving my citizenship?

I can vote and have
good credit, pay
all my bills. And
not use my credit cards
up So I can get things
on credit.

I can vote and have good credit, pay all my bills. And not use my credit cards up so I can get things on credit.

M

Citizenship

What are my goals for improving my citizenship?

I can be Independent by
do own things with no body
telling you my things are goi
college and driving license
by 16 if independent

I can be independent by do(ing) (my) own things with no body telling you my things are going to college and driving license by 16 if independent

F

Citizenship

What are my goals for improving my citizenship?

I am a great citizen. I get up for old people, Pregnant woman and people with injury, woman with kids even people who look tired. I hep people who need help. I hear some one ask me where did you get for example that oil I go take them there and they get it or I go get it. I am really a nice person but I got some problems like everyone else. But you never know like they say the grass is greener on the other side. My grass is Green

I am a great citizen. I get up for old people, pregnant woman and people with injury, woman with kids even people who look tired. I help people who need help. I hear some one ask me where did you get for example that oil (and) go take them there and they get it or I go get it. I am really a nice person but I got some problems like everyone else. But you never know like they say the grass is greener on the other side. My grass is <u>green</u>.

F

Citizenship

What are my goals for improving my citizenship?

Be More postively active in my community. For ex.

Start a girl's basketball team to raise money 4 more playgrounds, centers... etc.

Be more positively active in my community. For ex.

Start a girl's basketball team to raise money for more playgrounds, centers...etc.

M

Citizenship

What are my goals for improving my citizenship?

stope getin in trouble with the law

stop getting in trouble with the law

(Unknown)

Citizenship

What are my goals for improving my citizenship?

don't litter

don't litter

M

Citizenship

What are my goals for improving my citizenship?

By Stop getting in troble with the Law.

By stop getting in trouble with the law.

F

Citizenship

What are my goals for improving my citizenship?

My goals for improving my Citizenship is to make shure everything I do and have is legal. I also will try my best to vote each year. I will also do the little thing for example recycle.

My goals for improving my citizenship is to make sure everything I do and have is legal. I also will try my best to vote each year. I will also do the little thing(s) for example recycle.

(Unknown)

Citizenship

What are my goals for improving my citizenship?

My goals for improving my citizenship are obeying the law even if I dont like it.

My goals for improving my citizenship are obeying the law even if I don't like it.

F

Citizenship

What are my goals for improving my citizenship?

stop having kids / until I grow up.
explang how heard it is to take care of a child.
As a teenager

stop having kids / until I grow up.
explaining how hard it is to take care of a child as a teenager

(Unknown)

Citizenship

What are my goals for improving my citizenship?

To try and Not Litter to Continue
To Volenteer in Community Center
helping younger children Work
with Computers.

To try and not litter to continue to volunteer in community center helping younger children work with computers.

F

Citizenship

What are my goals for improving my citizenship?

When I get older I like to
become more involved in the community.
Like helping out people in need
as far as food, clothes, and a place
for them to live, Also help people that
are sick or blind, and give
forster children good homes.
and help babys with aids get
better and stay well and alive.

When I get older I (would) like to become more involved in the community. Like helping out people in need as far as food, clothes and a place for them to live, Also help people that are sick or blind, and give foster children good homes, and help babies with AIDS get better and stay well and alive.

Citizenship: *Commentary*

The vast majority of students needed to have 'citizenship' defined, a very sad indictment of our educational system (30). Nevertheless, most students responded positively to our explanation and gave the impression that we were now putting a word to what heretofore had been an unnamed concept, a concept however with which they were familiar and which they readily embraced, namely participation in a political world bigger than ourselves, our families and our neighborhoods. Just as most students eagerly anticipated when they would have jobs, so too most of them looked forward to when they would be old enough to vote and obtain a driving license.

With this assignment, I intended to draw attention to what should have already been an assumption: of course I want to improve my citizenship. The question is, What actions can I take now to improve my citizenship?

Chapter Three: Academic Goals

Language Arts *Student Papers*

F

What are Language Arts?

Reading & Writing.

U

What are Language Arts? the study of
Language Arts is ~~a~~ English literature

U

What are Language Arts?

language Arts are the study of new ways to know what words are.

U

What are Language Arts? Are a way to describe how you ~~feel~~ by writing in words

---

U

What are Language Arts?

How you present your voice

F **Why do we study Language Arts?**
Literitore.

U **Why do we study Language Arts?**
To know what every word we say mean.

M **Why do we study Language Arts?**
We study Language Arts because we want to know how to read, write, and comprehend.

U **Why do we study Language Arts?** To have better Communications with each other

M **Why do we study Language Arts?**
To be proficiint readers

U **Why do we study Language Arts?**
To speak better

Why do we study Language Arts?— To learn how to be adjusted

F to the outside. And know how to be a prof-
fessional to the outside world.

U Why do we study Language Arts?
We study Language arts to find
out words that we can use.

Why do we study Language Arts?

U We study Language Arts because it is the
language we speak in this country, and because
we need to know the language's history

M Why do we study Language Arts?
So we can camtanaet

Why do we study Language Arts?

F So I can learn to Read & write.
And understanding what I read

U

What are my goals in Language Arts?

my goals in Language are to be able to have a conversation with bigger words instead of cussing or little baby words.

F

What are my goals in Language Arts? - To know that wherever I go I can be respected and know that my mouth is always proper.

M

What are my goals in Language Arts?

To be able to write a 20 page Essay without Spelling Errors

U

What are my goals in Language Arts?

when I read and there's words I don't know I never try to figure out what they mean and when I see or hear the word again I regret that I didn't find out what it means.

M · What are my goals in Language Arts?
To learn how to write a decent ~~essy~~ essay

F · What are my goals in Language Arts? are to Study Poetry

F · What are my goals in Language Arts? I hope I could write good poetry.

What are my goals in Language Arts?
U · My goals in language Arts is for me to write better.

What are my goals in Language Arts?
F · to know what I'm am Reading about.

M They can make math interesting by using really money.

M **How can teachers make the study of Mathematics more interesting?** By useing money

---

M **How can teachers make the study of Mathematics more interesting?**

If they'd use food.

U **How can teachers make the study of Mathematics more interesting?**

Playing games at the same time

F **How can teachers make the study of Mathematics more interesting?** Teacher can make the study of Mathematicks more interesting by doin it to not by using the answer books.

U

How can teachers make the study of Mathematics more interesting?

By doing progects with shapes.

How can teachers make the study of Mathematics more interesting?

U

Use blocks or not overload you with stuff or else you will not learn it and not remember ~~it~~ the lesson.

How can teachers make the study of Mathematics more interesting? By making us have fun while we are learning it.

F

U

How can teachers make the study of Mathematics more interesting? Use it as A game

How can teachers make the study of Mathematics more interesting? Games.

F

F How can teachers make the study of Mathematics more interesting? by Playins and malkins them out of games

M How can teachers make the study of Mathematics more interesting? by makeing it more fun

F How can teachers make the study of Mathematics more interesting? By helping me understand. And beingpasent.

U How can teachers make the study of Mathematics more interesting? break it down in a simpler form so that people could understand it easier it's not that I stupid it's just a easier way out.

M How can teachers make the study of Mathematics more interesting?

Explain it better and relate it to real life situations.

M How can teachers make the study of Mathematics more interesting? by put math in a car game.

How can teachers make the study of Mathematics more interesting? by not getting their attitude when we ask them for help

F

How can teachers make the study of Mathematics more interesting?

U

have the kids teach for a day

U

How can teachers make the study of Mathematics more interesting? it is already interesting.

How can teachers make the study of Mathematics more interesting? Well they have to explain there self more. When they do math with me. Because of the simple fact that I hate math, and I need to learn it.

F

How can teachers make the study of Mathematics more interesting?

F

using word Problems more that have to do with the everyday life

M How can teachers make the study of Mathematics more interesting? Math Gamez

F How can teachers make the study of Mathematics more interesting?
Put food in the mist of it

U How can teachers make the study of Mathematics more interesting? taeking step by step

U How can teachers make the study of Mathematics more interesting? beyg akting it out

What is Social Studies?

U

things that happend in the past.

Why do we study Social Studies?

U

To learn of the Past and how it has become Now.

Why do we study Social Studies?

U

The reason why we study social studies is because there are more going on in the world then america.

Why do we study Social Studies?

F

so we can learn about our ancesters and the refigeens and the reson why the world is how it is today.

U **Why do we study Social Studies?** to learn more about our and other People's Cultures

Why do we study Social Studies?

U So we know whats going on in our world. cause you should know whats going on.

What questions do I have about Social Studies?

Why do we study Social Studies?

M To learn more about other cultures as well as our own.

Why do we study Social Studies? So we can learn what

F Happen in the past so we can prevent it from happening again

What questions do I have about Social Studies?

F I want to learn more about African American history.

What questions do I have about Social Studies?

F what are supposed to be learning exactly.

Science *Student Papers*

U

Why do we study Science?

We study science because it help us find cures for sick people.

F

Why do we study Science? To lean about our body

F

Why do we study Science? We study science to explore about life and it's wonders.

U

Why do we study Science? to help Better people

F **Why do we study Science?** So that we can no about the backrea and ilnesses in the world today and the planets and how the Earth got the way it is.

M **In Science, I enjoy learning about**

photosynthesis, metamorphesis, nucleus, biology

M **In Science, I enjoy learning about**

human antany.

F **In Science, I enjoy learning about** the female reproductive System.

U **I would like to learn more about**

I would like to learn more about the human body.

F **I would like to learn more about**

Fossils, is there any life on other Planets

U **I would like to learn more about**

How animals become different Kinds of animals.

M I would like to learn more about Bugs

F I would like to learn more about the brain cells

Notes and References

1. For comments on the origin and meaning of the word *psyche* see Philosophy of Education (Mazzullo, AuthorHouse 2012) p 21-22
2. I included the remark about spelling because I didn't want students to hesitate in using a word because they were unsure of its spelling, and to communicate to students that I anticipated possible difficulties with spelling and that I was more interested in what they had to say than in the accuracy of their spelling.
3. *Student Papers*; when italicized, refers specifically to the 900 papers that are the subject of this book. *Student Papers* refers exclusively to these primary, unaltered writings by students.
4. *Summary of Wishes* are the students' stated wishes, from all *Student Papers*; listed verbatim alphabetically.
5. *Commentary* throughout this work has been rather informal. I tried to touch on what I thought were some of the more interesting and important points. However, certainly there are items worthy of commentary that have not been included in my remarks.
6. I use the terminology *Academic Goals* somewhat loosely here. I included informational questions because I wanted to assess prerequisite knowledge relating to students' stated goals.
7. See for instance Participation in Goal Setting: Effects on Self-Efficacy and Skills of Learning-Disabled Children (Schunk '85, Journal of Special Education)
8. Sub-goals refer to component prerequisite goals. For instance, if a student wants to become a doctor, s/he first needs to get a high school diploma; we look at the child's transcript to see what courses s/he needs and we establish an immediate (sub) goal involving the completion of the required courses.
9. Philosophy of Education (Mazzullo, AuthorHouse 2012); references thereof will heretofore be abbreviated PhilEd.
10. When I Am 21 (underlined) refers to this book. When I Am 21, not underlined, refers to the title of *Student Papers* on this topic.
11. PhilEd p 41. 'Standard of living' encompasses the same ideas and values Adams addresses in his discussion of *The American Dream,* namely the attainment of physical, social, emotional, intellectual and spiritual health.

12. For discussions on the meaning and nature of happiness and fulfillment, see PhilEd especially Ch 1-2.
13. PhilEd p 30-32.
14. I have extended the standard definitions of concrete and abstract nouns to wishes, that is, a concrete wish is one that is perceivable by the senses whereas an abstract wish is not.
15. Except for illegible words, which I have followed in parentheses and italics with the intended word, I have recorded students' writings in all *Summary of Wishes* sections verbatim, in alphabetical order. I have not listed all the times exact phrases were repeated by students, (such as 'play in the NBA'), but I have included all variations, such as 'go to the NBA'.
16. PhilEd p 16
17. PhilEd p 109-111
18. Mother/mother figure: the term 'mother' is used to refer to the mother or the person who is filling the chief care-giving, parental role. It can refer to a father, to other family relative(s), or to an institution.
19. 'Good mother' refers to the image of whomever or whatever the person thinks of when imaging the original unconditional love from a mother or mother figure.
20. The sections on Cars and Money do not have a *Student Papers* section.
21. PhilEd p 111-113
22. PhilEd p 112
23. PhilEd p 17-18
24. PhilEd p 34-36
25. PhilEd p 19
26. PhilEd p 56
27. PhilEd p 46
28. PhilEd p 60
28. For the origins of this passage, see http://quoteinvestigator.com/2013/01/10/watch-your-thoughts/
29. PhilEd p xvii

About the Author

Mr. Mazzullo's ideas are influenced by a background in Philosophy (B.A., UC Berkeley), Special Education (M.A., Teachers College Columbia U) and Psychotherapy (Washington Square Institute NYC). Other academic interests include history, religion, literature and the classics.

Contributing to Mr. Mazzullo's philosophy and values are +30 years working with inner-city special education students. When I Am 21 is an account of his experience in a residential center for abused children, told in the students' own words, expressed as wishes for themselves 'if you could wish for anything for when you become 21 years old'.

One of the author's intentions with When I Am 21 is to complement his first book Philosophy of Education (Mazzullo, AuthorHouse 2012) in an effort to show where the academic disciplines of Psychology and Philosophy intersect with expressed student wishes, as these wishes reflect and inform so much of the content of Philosophy of Education.

Mr. Mazzullo is licensed in New York State to teach Elementary Education, Mathematics and Special Education, to serve as School Administrator and Supervisor, and to practice Psychotherapy.

His hobbies include gardening, cooking, reading and bicycling. He has been retired from teaching since the summer of 2010, and he spends a considerable amount of time at the family beach house in North Carolina, where he does a lot of his writing. His wife and three children are all teachers in the New York metropolitan area.

Mr. Mazzullo encourages readers to visit his web-site http://www.louismazzullo.com where comments and questions are welcome.